And That's the Way It Will Be

Christopher Harper

And That's the Way It Will Be

News and Information in a Digital World

 New York University Press

New York and London

NEW YORK UNIVERSITY PRESS
New York and London

Library of Congress Cataloging-in-Publication Data
Harper, Christopher, 1951–
And that's the way it will be : news and information in a
digital world / Christopher Harper.
p. cm.
Includes bibliographical references and index.
ISBN 0-8147-3576-2 (alk. paper)
1. Journalism—Data processing.   2. Electronic periodicals.
3. Information networks.   I. Title.
PN4784.E5H36   1998
070.4'0285—dc21   97-45351
                              CIP

New York University Press books are printed on acid-free paper,
and their binding materials are chosen for strength and durability.

Manufactured in the United States of America

10 9 8 7 6 5 4 3 2 1

contents

Contents

Five-year-old Cecylia is stumped. She's gotten the little creatures onto the ship and marched them to the bridges. If she
puts the creatures on the wrong bridge, it sneezes and comes
tumbling down, stranding them. But she gets them all through
safely. The next stop, the cave, has always been easy because
the four sentries guarding the entrance usually let the strange-
looking "Zoombinis" pass. So Cecylia moves Auldea, who has
blue hair, a blue nose, and a coiled spring for feet, toward the
next stop with fifteen of her friends. But the pizza troll does
not like the toppings Cecylia selects for the pizza pie and
won't let the creatures past. "More toppings please," the troll
complains. She chooses cheese, mushrooms, and anchovies.
That makes the difference. "The perfect pizza," the troll ex-
claims as he lets the little creatures go to the rest stop. Neisu,
a droopy-eyed, blue-nosed girl on roller skates, makes it
through, as does Laupy, a boy with a purple nose that matches
his purple shoes.

Cecylia is playing The Logical Journey of the Zoombinis, a
computer game that stresses logical thinking and mathematics.
It's fun, too. The Zoombinis lost their home in paradise to the
big bad Blotes and are trying to find a new place to live. The

path can be difficult and dangerous, but Cecylia tries to help the Zoombinis along the way.

Cecylia is my daughter. She belongs to a new generation of "digerati" who will use a computer during their lifetime for news, information, entertainment, and education. "Daddy, I want to use the computer," she announced one day after watching me spend hour after hour on my Macintosh Performa. It didn't take long for her to figure out how to load a CD-ROM, click on the icon, and start off on her own, experiencing far greater control over activities organized by her parents or teachers. She could choose where she wanted to go, what she wanted to draw, how she wanted to play, and when she wanted to stop.

Remember the first time you touched a computer? For me it wasn't much fun. In 1974, I was working as an editor and reporter for the Associated Press in Chicago while attending graduate school at Northwestern University. The AP installed one of the first computer systems in the news business. Behind glass doors in an air-conditioned room, the computers often crashed at the worst possible times. Back then, the system did not automatically back up copies of the story being edited or written. If you had a story open and had not copied it, you could kiss it goodbye. The editors worked on what were called VDTs—video display terminals—or CRTs—cathode-ray tubes. The machines had no diskettes. There was no memory on the individual machines, only on the huge computers behind the glass partitions. Some reporters simply refused to use the VDTs, particularly the old hands. That's how my love-hate relationship with computers began. I *remember* trying to close a file before it got sent into eternal cyberspace. (Of course, it was a decade before author William Gibson coined the word "cyberspace." At the time, I did not realize that visionary Robert Metcalfe had just finished his thesis on creating networks.)

For the past twenty-four years, I have struggled to come to

grips with my relationship with computers. I've used Macs and IBMs. I even learned how to operate a digital editing system for video. I am not a computer geek. When I teach people how to use computers, I refer to the class as driver's education. The computer is like an automobile. The object of the exercise is to get from one place to another. Look how profoundly the automobile changed the world in which we live in both good and bad ways. Independence. Smog. Dying inner cities. Glistening new suburbs. Cheaper goods and services. Dying railroads. The computer also will profoundly affect the way people live both in good and bad ways. Keep in mind that Alexander Graham Bell, a speech teacher, was trying to create a hearing aid for his wife when he invented the telephone. Thomas Edison was convinced that his invention, which became known as the phonograph, would help people dictate instructions and memoirs, not play recordings. So it's difficult to predict what impact computers will actually have.

Nearly twenty years ago, my wife Elizabeth and I left the center of news and information, Washington, D.C., for Lebanon, where civil war had decimated the communications system. I used a telex—a machine somewhere between Morse code and today's computer—to file my stories for *Newsweek*. Because the cost of sending a message on the telex was rather expensive, you did not receive many missives unless it was important. That meant that people provided you with important, not useless, information or questions. The telephones in Lebanon worked only occasionally, and they were even more expensive to use. That meant the journalists in Lebanon and the Middle East could actually report stories without significant daily interference from the bosses in New York—a rarity today with cellular telephones and other devices that make communications instantaneous throughout much of the world. In Iraq, I had to register my typewriter with the government because the portable machine was considered "a potential tool for revolution." (Ironically, even Saddam Hussein now has his own Web page.) In Egypt, after four days without telephone communications, I finally yelled in the receiver: "If you are going to tap the phone, at least you can make it work." About an hour later, a man called up. "Mr. Harper, your telephone is repaired." Today, many governments want to censor the Internet because it does pose a huge threat when people can obtain information easily and without the censorship of the local dictator.

This book's intention is to look at computers as a means of providing and receiving news and information in the age of the Internet. Looking forward and making predictions about digital journalism can prove difficult. When I asked Neil Budde, the editor of the *Wall Street Journal Interactive Edition*, how news and information will change by the year 2000, he said: "You must be kidding! I can't tell you what's going to happen by the end of the year." Roger Ailes, the president of Fox Television, put it simply, "Anybody who says he knows what's going to happen is b.s.-ing you." I often say that those who predict the future of news and information in a digital age are stupid, lying, or Bill Gates, the only man with enough money to influence what is going to happen. I suppose I may be underlining my lack of intelligence by undertaking this project because I assure you I am neither lying nor Bill Gates.

This book is dedicated to my daughter, Cecylia, whose life will be dramatically influenced by computers, and my wife, Elizabeth, who has been my fellow traveler and able critic as we lived in six cities on four continents over the past two decades as a result of my work for *Newsweek* and ABC. I also thank the more than one hundred people who spoke with me about digital journalism. I want to thank New York University Press and its director, Niko Pfund, for having confidence in this project.

chapter one

A Road Map to the Information Superhighway

The illiterate of the 21st century will not be those who cannot read and write, but those who cannot learn, unlearn, and relearn.   —Alvin Toffler,
author of *Future Shock*

Mother's Day 1997. The temperature hovered around seventy degrees in New York City, but a brisk wind made it clear that summer had not yet arrived. In the contests that pitted human versus human, the New York Yankees won; the New York Rangers defeated the New Jersey Devils; the New York Knicks downed the Miami Heat; and even the New York Mets won. It is a rare day when all New York teams win. But in a cramped room in midtown Manhattan, the battle pitted human against machine. It was the final game of six between world chess champion Garry Kasparov and a computer, IBM's Deep Blue. The two stood tied after the first five games.

In little more than a hour, the machine had defeated the finest chess player in history. Kasparov's fans hissed at the notion that the machine had won. In recent years computers have replaced humans working on car assembly lines, and machines have enabled companies to downsize workforces at major corporations. Now, in head-to-head competition, the machine had won, too.

Deep Blue's victory over Kasparov seemed somewhat reminiscent of the legend about the African American railroad worker John Henry. Recalled in fable and song, Henry tested his strength against an automated steam hammer. Henry defeated the machine, but he died from exertion. Is another machine, the computer, to be feared? Have we reached the dreaded 1984 simply a few years later than expected? Will the computer ultimately determine what we need to know in the age of digital news and information?

For nearly two decades, many Americans got their news from one man: Walter Cronkite. We cried with him on the day John F. Kennedy died. We celebrated with him when men landed on the moon. We believed him when he determined Vietnam was a war that could not be won. We listened as he explained how the Watergate burglary lead directly to the White House. We watched as he counted the number of days Americans had been held hostage in Iran. And every night we listened as he signed off the broadcast: "And that's the way it is."

Today, many Americans under the age of thirty don't have a clue who Walter Cronkite is. For them, that's the way it was, and it's time to move on. It's difficult to disagree, particularly when the venerable ex-newsman, now in his eighties, complains that the Internet could be a "frightful danger to all of us."[1] His evidence: an apparently fake document purporting that U.S. military missiles had accidentally shot down TWA Flight 800, which crashed after takeoff on July 17, 1996. Dozens of reputable journalists dismissed the document for what it was, a fake. Yet another seasoned journalist bought the story hook, line, and sinker—Pierre Salinger, formerly of ABC News.

The Internet does pose a frightful danger to the way journalists for decades have reported news, keeping the public away from original documents, records, and sources. The Internet provides many readers and viewers as much, if not more, information than many journalists, who still shudder at the thought of using the new technology. Journalism had best get used to the new medium. Cronkite's role seemed appropriate during a certain period in the nation's history, when families gathered around the television every evening to watch the news. That's the way it was. Today and tomorrow, digital journalism is the way it will be.

A while ago, a commission to study the media found that the advertising-based, commercial character of the media and the attendant quest for maximum audience left them vulnerable to demands of private interests and public pressure groups. The concentration of ownership had effectively removed competition while increasing profits, to the point where the proprietors of the media were now in the upper-income brackets and tended to reflect the views of the privileged classes. The report continued that the mass media upon which a great majority of people depended emphasized the exceptional rather than the representative, the sensational rather than the significant. "The result is not a continued story of the life of a people but a series of vignettes made to seem more significant than they really are." Sound familiar? Robert Hutchins, then the president of the University of Chicago, finished this report fifty years ago. The media attacked the report as either desiring communist or fascist control of the press. Hutchins's ideas should be analyzed again for their prescience and insight as we move into the next millennium.

Will digital journalism be any different? That's what this book is about. The current structure seems to be failing, turning off people who should know what is going on. This book is intended to provide information about where digital journalism is today and where it *may* go. Digital journalism has great promise. It is the best chance those in the profession and those who seek and use information have to get back on track. If this doesn't work, we will simply isolate ourselves into our own little niches, where confrontation, comment, and community will have no place. We will simply become egocentric and distant from one another.

I focus first on myriad audiences that exist for the media, and how many people aren't exactly pleased with traditional news and information sources. Then I will profile some of the key players in the world of digits. Then there are three chapters about digital journalism and how it's done well and poorly, including a look at the *New York Times*, the *Chicago Tribune*, and MSNBC. Somehow someone will have to pay for all of this, so I look at advertisers, subscribers, and a few other methods of making money on news and information in a digital age. After that, there are three chapters on the upside, downside, and the dark side of the Internet. The upside focuses on news and information in poor neighborhoods and the developing world. The downside examines a host of troubles the Internet faces, from hackers to speed. And the dark side discusses the issues of pornography, hate, and privacy on the Internet's news and information system. Then I turn to whether government will leave us alone on the Internet. Finally, what would a book like this be without predictions? So we will start at the beginning and end on the future.

Bear in mind that news and information, let alone computers, are actually quite new. If you consider the time frame of human life on earth and imagine it as a twenty-four-hour day, the information age is a fraction of that day. The invention of speech, which occurred about 100,000 years B.C., would not take place until 9:30 P.M. Writing occurred about eight minutes before midnight. The ability to store and transmit speech and writing electronically through the telegraph, telephone, radio, and television happened about eleven seconds before midnight. The digital computer just made it under the wire: two seconds before midnight in our communication day.[2]

Media futurist and long-time new media specialist Roger Fidler thinks the introduction of computer language may be as significant as the introduction of speech and written languages. "When discussing communication technologies, two agents of change stand out above all others—spoken language and written language. Each has vastly expanded the human communication system and played a central role in the advancement and spread of civilization," he writes. "Now a new and quite different class

5

of language—digital language—is emerging as yet another agent of change."[3]

So why are so many people afraid of the digital age? Because it's new and *means* change? Because it seems complicated? Because ten-year-old kids understand more about computers and the Internet than many adults do? The answers to these questions are yes. Nevertheless, few people give a second thought about operating a far more complicated and far more dangerous piece of equipment than a computer every day. It's called an automobile. When a car crashes, it can be deadly. A computer weighs a few pounds. When a computer crashes, it's only annoying. A computer really can't hurt you that much except maybe through increased eye strain or pains in the hand. Drivers on an actual highway can kill you.

Granted, the automobile has become much easier to use than a computer. Nearly everyone who buys a car can drive. But imagine if General Motors had a help line for people who bought automobiles but didn't know how to drive:

Help line: General Motors help line, how can I help you?

Customer: Hi! I just bought my first car, and I chose your car because it has automatic transmission, cruise control, power steering, power brakes, and power door locks.

Help line: Thanks for buying our car. How can I help you?

Customer: How do I work it?

Help line: Do you know how to drive?

Customer: Do I know how to *what*?

Help line: Do you know how to *drive*?

Customer: I'm not a technical person! I just want to go places in my car!

The digital age stands as part of a historical continuum to learn and use information effectively. An abacus—a wooden rack holding beads on parallel wires—apparently ranked as the first known calculating device when it appeared 2,000 years ago in China. Blaise Pascal built the first calculating machine in 1642. It performed addition to help Pascal's father, a tax collector in

France. Charles Babbage, a mathematics professor at Cambridge, determined that lengthy computations, especially those for mathematical tables, consisted of repeated operations. Babbage designed a calculating machine, which he called a "difference engine." With backing from the British government, Babbage started in 1823 to build a steam-powered calculator. But he never finished his computer, primarily because he lost interest and there was little economic need for the machine. Almost everyone, however, credits Babbage with providing the basic design for today's computers. In 1890, Herman Hollerith developed machines for the U.S. Census Bureau that automatically read information punched into cards. The process greatly reduced errors and enhanced productivity. For years, punched-card machines performed the bulk of computer for business and science. Hollerith's business, Tabulating Machine Company, ultimately became IBM.

7

The modern computer to process information had many fathers, but the idea man was Vannevar Bush. During World War II, Bush, an engineer from the Massachusetts Institute of Technology, performed what many considered a miracle. Bush got more than six thousand scientists to cooperate, share information, and forge research links during the war. As head of the Office of Scientific Research and Development, Bush was, in essence, the first science advisor to the president. Bush was hardly a bureaucrat. Just before the war, he invented a forerunner of the modern computer, the "differential analyzer," which could do complicated mathematical calculations without making mistakes.

As World War II wound down, Bush looked ahead. He wanted his fellow scientists to find ways to use technology to better the human race rather than destroy it. In a July 1945 article in the *Atlantic Monthly* entitled, "As We May Think," Bush outlined his agenda for what would become the computer. He called it "memex."

Consider a future device for individual use, which is a sort of mechanized private file and library. It needs a name, and to coin one at random, "memex" will do. A memex is a device in which an individual stores all his books, records, and communications and which is mechanized so that it may be consulted with exceeding speed and flexibility. It is an enlarged intimate supplement to his memory. It consists of a desk, and while it can presumably be operated from a distance, it is primarily the piece of furniture at which he works. On the top are slanting translucent screens, on which material can be projected for convenient reading. There is a keyboard, and sets of buttons and levers.[4]

8

The next year, the first electronic digital computer was born at the Moore School of Electronic Engineering of the University of Pennsylvania. Its name was ENIAC, short for "Electrical Numerical Integrator And Calculator." ENIAC occupied 1,800 square feet of floor space and had far less power than today's portable computer. ENIAC consumed about 180,000 watts of electrical power. That's about 4,500 light bulbs. ENIAC performed calculations about a thousand times faster than previous computer designs. The first generation of modern programmed electronic computers used random access memory (RAM). This memory, which is still used today, could provide almost constant access to any piece of information randomly. That means you can find information anywhere from page 1 to 257 rather than leafing through the book from the beginning to find page 212. RAM increased from 8,000 bits to 64,000 bits in commercial machines in the early 1960s. Today's typical desktop computer has 100 to 200 times more power to process a far wider array of information, including words, graphics, audio, and video.

Nearly everyone in the United States knows the word "Internet." But how many people can actually explain what it is? In 1969, the Pentagon's Advanced Research Projects Agency four computer sites comprised the network named "ARPANET." Boys being boys—nearly all of the scientists were men—ARPANET became an electronic post office. Researchers did use the network to collaborate on projects and talk about work, but much of the time the scientists gossiped and schmoozed. A subscriber could send an identical message to a large number of network subscribers—the first time that news and information could be shared over such a digital network. While computer administrators frowned upon such uses of the network, the scientists turned increasingly to chat groups. One of the first, SF-LOVERS, connected science fiction fans with one another so they could share information about their favorite authors. Twenty years later, the general public joined in.

9

So when will the digital age enter the mainstream? Some may point with fear to the victory of IBM's chess master as the beginning of the end. For me, however, the era entered the mainstream on a more positive note on October 26, 1996, game six of the World Series between the New York Yankees and the Atlanta Braves. For years, a blimp from Goodyear, the Rust Belt tire company, provided panoramic, videotaped pictures of important sporting events throughout the country. But severe winds had battered Goodyear's blimp, and it couldn't fly that day. Enter AltaVista, the Internet company, to save the day. As the Yankees claimed the world championship that night, the digital age entered the mainstream—a shared experience of human and machine—as millions of television viewers watched the Internet blimp pinch hit for the Rust Belt blimp, the symbol of the old superhighway of asphalt and concrete.

The Audience: Who Wants News and Information in a Digital World and Why?

Kids have little computer bodies with disks that store information. They remember who had to do the dishes the last time you had spaghetti, who lost the knob off the TV set six years ago, who got punished for teasing the dog when he wasn't teasing the dog, and who had to wear the girl boots the last time it snowed.

—Erma Bombeck

Jessica Daneshvar does not like the colors she's chosen for the fishbowl on her computer screen. The dark-haired, four-year-old figures out what is wrong. The water's orange. So she takes the computer mouse and clicks on a blue electronic crayon to fix the color. Jessica then finds the print command and sends her design to a color printer nearby. When the picture, entitled "My Masterpiece," is done, she races proudly to her mother with the finished product at a computer training program in Ossining, New York. After her mother accepts the picture, Jessica scurries back to her desk. "I just want her to be comfortable with the computer as a friendly tool," says Diana Daneshvar, a nurse and mother of four. "I don't want her to get too gung-ho. You want her to do so much, but you have to remember she's just a kid," Daneshvar adds. "Jessica really likes to have things that she can control."

Control. That's what attracts many kids to computers. Think about it. How much can a child actually control during the course of a day? A child can tell the computer what he or she wants it to do. Meet the new generation of digerati for whom computers will be the primary means of news, information, and entertainment.

Teacher Diana MacLean follows a motto. "You gotta have fun or you can't be here," says MacLean of Futurekids, a national network of more than 200 computer training outlets for children. "A child has to explore and make mistakes." MacLean, who

holds a graduate degree in education, teaches children starting at age three. Today, she has a group of four-year-olds who usually work in teams of two. The one-hour session concentrates on a variety of skills. First, the children take a CD-ROM from its holder and carefully place the program into the computer. Justin and Daniel select Bailey's Book House, a program that helps them write a story. Justin wants Harley the horse to be the main character, so the four-year-old clicks the computer mouse on Harley. A voice announces, "This is a story about Harley." Justin and Daniel follow a series of options that allow the children to construct a personalized story. In this saga of derring-do, Harley goes on a ride in a bathtub to the city. The two boys are oblivious to the teacher. Many of the youngsters have spent only six hours on the computers—one hour a week. Jessica and Michelle are working nearby on a program, Jack's House. The CD-ROM program allows the girls to select different parts of a house. They decide to cultivate Jack's garden and plant some electronic flowers. Austin wants to work by himself with Sammy's Science House and prints out a caterpillar. Each child scans and uses three programs. The hour goes by quickly, and no one wants to leave.

Today, students from kindergarten through high school have the greatest access to news and information via computer of any other generation. In schools, nearly seven out of ten children have access to a computer and six out of ten have access to the Internet. Take, Lyssette Cruz, for example, one of the new digerati. She is strictly business. She has a newspaper to publish, and the staff is behind schedule. "How should I conclude this?" asks reviewer Tiffany Cirighiano as she shows a suggestion to Cruz. "That's fine," Lyssette barks back. Angela Soto is putting the final touches on a readership poll. Raymond Torres is rewriting an article that didn't pass muster. The *Trimester*, the newspaper at Holy Name School on Manhattan's Upper West Side, is scheduled to hit the stands soon. The seventh-grade class writes and edits all the stories by computer. Layout and printing are also done by computer.

The school's students come mostly from working-class families with limited incomes. Fifty-five percent of the 600 students—pre-kindergarten to eighth grade—is Hispanic. Thirty-five percent is Haitian, and the remaining 20 percent is mostly African American. Through a combination of grants, donations, and fees, Holy Name has assembled an impressive network of ninety machines. "These are not wealthy kids," says Richard Grieco, the principal at Holy Name. "But there's no reason they should not have access to the future." Hortensia Dominquez heads the computer laboratory at Holy Name. "If we have a discipline problem, all we have to say is you won't be going to computer class today," she says. "The problem's over. They love it here."

Computers, more than newspapers, magazines, or television, interest the students at Holy Name. While every one of the forty-two seventh graders at Holy Name uses a computer, less than half reads a newspaper. Many get news from local television stations. Fewer than one of four listens to radio news. Cable News Network (CNN), C-SPAN, and National Public Radio rank as the least likely places for the students to obtain news. News magazines such as *Time*, *Newsweek*, and *U.S. News & World Report*—once staples for most students-—are read regularly by less than 10 percent of those surveyed at Holy Name. What interests these twelve- and thirteen-year-olds? Health, entertainment, crime, and famous people rank as the four highest-rated news categories by the students. News events about Washington rank number eleven, followed by local government. The coverage of business and finance ranks next to the bottom, while consumer news comes in last. Twelve-year-old Manouchka Ashley Daniel follows reports on crime, particularly incidents in her neighborhood. She reads about health issues pertaining to women, such as breast cancer. Politics turns her off. She shows me a letter she has written to New York governor George Pataki, attacking his decision to lay off state workers. Unlike a majority of young people who pass up international news, she reads about Haiti, where her relatives live. She complains about "media stereotypes" of the Haitians as prone to violence and carriers of AIDS. Manouchka adds: "I want some news that's good. Let's talk about the good things. Everything you hear about New York is bad."

For the digerati at Holy Name, the focus is clearly local. When the school's newspaper hits the stands, it includes the seventh-grade class bidding farewell to the graduating eighth graders. There is a student poll on favorite vacation spots, a review of the school play, and even recipes for hot fudge sundaes and other not-so-healthy treats. Digital gurus should take note from those of the new digerati: the edition is filled with local, local, and more local news.

Teenagers still watch television a lot and talk on the telephone, but 98 percent of them have used a computer and spend an average of more than four hours a week using one.[1] One in two teenagers said they could easily live without a VCR, and one in three said they could live without a television. But it appears they cannot live without their computers. Only slightly more than two in ten said they could give up their computer. Officials estimate about 18.8 million U.S. kids under age eighteen have access to home computers.

A few other facts about the teenage cybergeneration:

Nine out of ten teens have written a report for school using a word processing program.

Nearly six out of ten have used the Internet to do research for a school project.

Nearly five out of ten have chatted on the Internet or sent e-mail.

Nearly eight out of ten said they would prefer using the Internet for school projects to using books and magazines.

More than eight out of ten said they think they won't make a good living unless they have computer skills and understand other technological developments.

What about the older kids? More than thirty million Americans comprise Generation X (a term applied to those in their twenties that many of them hate). When it comes to news and information, what exactly do they want? During a typical week, many young adults read the Sunday paper and at least one newspaper during the week.[2] Newspapers do remain the primary source for local news and in-depth information. Regular readers in this age group describe newspapers as easy to use. That's the good news. The bad news? Nearly half of these young adults says they could get along just fine without reading a newspaper.

Who exactly are GenXers? So far, this groups seems branded as a bunch of selfish underachievers with a penchant toward bad music and Satanic practices. Not surprisingly, the popular definition bears little resemblance to the truth. Actually, this group is about as diverse as they come. In fact, at least four distinct groups exist with different tastes in news and information. The first group represents about four in ten GenXers who are predominantly female, including a large concentration of African and Hispanic Americans who are likely to be parents—often single parents. They raise their families on the lowest personal income among GenXers. Yet these GenXers are practical, hardworking homebodies with a hunger for romance and fashion, which can translate into reading and viewing habits about famous people and trends. The second group includes slightly fewer than three out of ten of this generation who are older and the most likely to be married. They are highly educated and driven by faith, not success. One out of two is religious. One in four describes himself or herself as a born-again Christian. This group believes in itself, the nation, and God. Here, the reading and viewing habits coalesce into more traditional types of news and information: politics, community news, and sports. About two out of ten consider their lifestyle more important than a career. For this third group, there is no right or wrong way to live; pleasure is important. A fourth group, which represents fewer than two out of ten GenXers, are predominantly male and heavily concentrated in the South. They are drifters, escapists who yearn for security and status, identifying with brands and products that offer a sense of belonging and self-esteem. Those who live for the moment and those who yearn for security and status tend toward news and information about entertainment and trends.

What does Generation X want? No simple answer exists. More and more have turned to the computer to access the Internet and the World Wide Web rather than using conventional media. "Does everybody care about what's going on? Yeah. Actually, they do care," says one young computer designer. "Why doesn't everybody watch the news? Because they don't care about *that* news. I see several problems with news—context, relevance, and sensationalism. When I watch the evening news, I am appalled at what I see."

Among young adults, many Internet users hold strong opinions about education, the deficit, health care, and politics. Polls showed many voted in the November 1996 elections. "The fact that educational issues and balancing the federal budget were two of the top three issues in the minds of our audience tells me that the transition generation is a lot more sophisticated than many are willing to admit," argues chief executive officer Bo Peabody of Tripod, the company that conducted the survey.[3]

Many want a sense of community. But that community may not mean people in the same town or even of the same age. Community means a place where people share common bonds and interests. GenXers' sense of cultural identity relates closely to the communities they choose to belong to. Because of technology, virtual communities exist today that make it possible for new and enhanced means of communications. "Virtual communities will not only change the nature of communications but will almost change the profile of the audience," the survey found.

Another study, funded by Merrill Lynch, found that one in five GenXers uses the Internet daily, among the highest rates in all age groups. The findings strongly suggest that on-line publishers should target this group. "The more that you can gear your efforts toward the Gen-X crowd, and then expand up into the baby boom, the greater your payoff is going to be," argues Pete Snyder of Luntz Research Companies, which conducted the study for Merrill Lynch. "If I were involved with an on-line publication, I would aim for the younger crowd—that is where the fish are—and have it swell upwards. As that generation grows and the generations come after it, the implications are going to be pretty amazing."[4]

Are on-line users a bunch of techno-geeks who cut their teeth on video games and hacked into Defense Department computers? Hardly. More than thirty million adults use on-line services in the United States, according to a recent survey by FIND/SVP. Another ten million on-line users are under eighteen years old, including six million who go on-line at home and another four million who do so at school.[5] By the year 2000, the number of adults on-line is expected to reach sixty million. Users of the Internet parallel the rough demographics of the nation as a whole. Whites comprise 86 percent of the total users versus 85 percent of the general public. Nonwhites stand at 14 percent of the Internet users, the same percentage in the general population, although Asians tend to use the Internet at a higher rate and Hispanics at a lower rate. African Americans comprise 9 percent of Internet users versus 10 percent of the general population.[6] The average age of all the World Wide Web users is thirty-four. More than four out of ten people on the Internet are female, a significant change in recent years.[7] Education levels run somewhat

higher among Internet users: two out of three have attended college. Income levels are slightly higher than the general population, but those with incomes between $30,000 and $50,000 still
use the Internet in higher percentages than their representation
in the general population. Those who earn under $30,000 are less
likely to use the Internet, although the median income of those
using on-line services has been dropping significantly, to
$48,000—an indication that not only the wealthy have decided
to join the digital generation.[8]

"The Internet is quickly developing a serious audience that
views on-line content on a consistent basis either at home or in
the workplace," according to the Wirthlin Report in September
1996.[9] The Internet appears to have reached a rate of adoption in
the United States—roughly 10 to 25 percent of its total market—
that should mean the system will gain users even faster than the
past few years.[10] Moreover, the amount of information the average American gets from electronic sources has been increasing
by 8 percent every ten years since 1960, while the amount of
information from printed sources has been stagnant.[11] Electronic
information is faster and cheaper to deliver. In fact, average citizens get about half of their news and entertainment from television. A.C. Nielsen estimates that the average household
television set is turned on for slightly more than seven hours a
day. Radio is second at about two hours a day, mainly during
commuting times. Estimates of newspaper reading vary from
eighteen to forty-nine minutes a day, while people read magazines from six to thirty minutes a day. Reading books averages
about eighteen minutes daily.[12] At work, there is no accurate comparison of what the new medium replaces except perhaps work.
At home, however, the computer user often watches less television and listens to the radio more.

No single profile exists for how someone uses the Internet for
news and information. Am I a typical Internet user? No. What

19

the computer allows me to do, however, is to work from home because I have access to all the news and information I need at the click of a mouse. Since I began to work, I have had to be physically present. The first job I had was when I was twelve, mowing lawns during the summer with a friend. At fourteen, I worked as a busboy in a restaurant. At seventeen, I shoveled cow manure in what's known as a "sale barn" in Wyoming, where cattle were bought and sold. At nineteen, I drove a truck, delivering stationery. At twenty, I worked in a sawmill, pulling lumber off a production line. From the ages of twenty-one to forty-three, I worked for a variety of news organizations—the Associated Press, *Newsweek* magazine, ABC News, and ABC 20/20. For all these jobs, I had to be somewhere other than my home. Computers have changed that for me. Almost every day for the past two years, my routine has been different. I still get up at 7 A.M. I still take a shower and dress. But now I sit down at my computer at home, and I have access to far more information than I ever had going into an office. A reporter still has to go out and see the scene, sniff the air, and find out what's happening. But I am far better prepared today by accessing the Internet than I ever was before, primarily because of the information I have available to me.

My first stop: electronic mail. That may include comments from colleagues. That may include assignments or questions from my students at Ithaca College, where I teach. I have canceled my subscription to the *New York Times* because I can receive all the articles I want from the Internet edition. I check the front page, sports, and a special section on the Internet, called Cyber Times. In the Personal Edition of the *Wall Street Journal*, I check my family's stock portfolio, including current holdings and values of each investment we have. That way I can determine whether we should make any trades before the market opens. Next stop, two personal editions of news and information from Infobeat and Individual Inc. I have submitted profiles to these two services that provide me with articles on international affairs, technology, and serendipitous features. I even get a service that tells me the weather for the next three days. Within forty-five minutes, I have an understanding of what's happening in the news, computers, and technology. If I want to read the *Washington Post*, the *Chicago Tribune*, the *Los Angeles Times*, or any of the more than 1,000 on-line publications in the world, it's easy. I simply go to each site with a click of the mouse. These are newspapers I saw only occasionally in New York. *HotWired* and *Salon*, two electronic magazines, land on my computer doorstep as does information from a variety of computer publications. I only have to ask once, and it is delivered to me on-line.

Then I tackle another aspect of news and information—the world of research by plugging into libraries throughout the world. Simply put, I do not surf the Internet. I'd drown. I use the Internet to find something I want to know. It's a target, not an amorphous wave. If I want to be entertained, that exists. If I want sex chat, that exists, too, as do kinky pictures and bizarre news groups. But more on that later (chapter 10).

Why do other people go on-line? The most important reason for one in three people who use the Internet is to send electronic mail, the most popular function on the Internet. But nearly as many use the Internet and the World Wide Web for research. One in six is simply curious, while roughly the same number look for specific news and information. One in eight wants business and financial information. One in twelve goes to the Internet for hobbies and entertainment, and roughly the same number travels into cyberspace for work and education. Chat rooms are popular for one in sixteen people. About the same number want to receive computer information. A small number of users go on-line to download computer software or to seek travel and sports information.

Those who want on-line news form a large group between eighteen and fifty years old, including many college graduates.[13] One significant reason many people are going on-line for news and information may be because traditional media are not meeting the needs of readers and listeners. Throughout the country, many people, but particularly computer users, are not satisfied with reading newspapers and watching television news. Slightly more than half of Internet users watch television news. That's down significantly in only one year. Slightly less than half of Internet users read a daily newspaper. Some may interpret those figures to mean computer users are simply ill-informed. That would be a mistake. On-line users spend as much time seeking information as those who do not own a computer. Simply put, many people are getting information from the Internet rather than the evening news. That is particularly true for those under fifty years old.

Nearly seven out of ten people think it is important to know what is in the news, mainly those over the age of fifty. That falls to four out of ten for those under the age of thirty, and only three out of ten under the age of thirty follow the news every day.[14] "A critical segment of the 'news of the future' audience does not have the basic level of interest to be engaged with the news," says a recent survey. And those who do are turning to the Internet, while the traditional readers of newspapers and viewers of television news are growing increasingly older. "The habit of picking up the daily newspaper religiously is found only among those over 50," the survey also says. "Network television news is joining newspapers as a medium for older citizens. . . . TV network news may be in danger of becoming an anachronism in the next century."[15]

What do people want to know about?[16] Crime stories interested all age groups in recent surveys, and these reports received the highest rating among all age groups. Four out of ten people

News Interests by Age (percentage of U.S. population)

	Total	18–29	30–49	50+
1. Crime	41	43	39	40
2. Local community	35	28	36	39
3. Health	34	27	29	45
4. Sports	26	30	24	24
5. Local government	24	14	22	32
6. Science & technology	20	19	20	19
7. Religion	17	12	13	26
8. Political news	16	10	13	22
9. International affairs	15	10	11	24
10. Entertainment	15	24	13	12
11. Consumer news	14	12	12	18
12. Business & finance	13	10	13	15
13. Famous people	13	16	10	15
14. Culture/the arts	10	9	9	11

SOURCE: Pew Research Center for the People & the Press.

ranked crime as what most interested them, with much the same results among those in three groups—those eighteen to twenty-nine years old, those thirty to forty-nine, and those over fifty. All groups have roughly the same interest in sports and science, but after that the taste in news varies widely between those under fifty and those over fifty. Many media outlets cater to the older, not the younger, audience. For example, less than two out of ten of those between eighteen and twenty-nine ranked local government news as important, while two out of ten of those thirty to forty-nine ranked local news as important. More than three out of ten of those over fifty ranked local government as important. Those over fifty ranked health, local government, religion, politics, and international news as important far more often than those under fifty. Younger people, particularly those eighteen to twenty-nine, showed greater interest in entertainment.

Crime does make the front pages and often is a major story on many local television newscasts. Simply put, if it bleeds, it leads. But take a look at the structure of most television news broadcasts. Government stories—be they local, state, national, or international—often dominate the first segment of the news. The survey clearly shows that people have limited interest in these stories. If there is interest, those over fifty tend to have greater interest than those who are younger.

On local broadcasts, the weather usually follows the news. Weather does not even hit the news radar screen for many people, but weather occupies a major part of most broadcasts even when no significant story happens. Sports usually follows the weather. Sports does interest most groups, particularly younger viewers. Newspapers tend to stress political news on the front page, leaving many younger readers scurrying for other sections. But what comes next? The metropolitan section. Again, older readers find interesting stories here, but younger readers generally do not. The next section usually is sports, which interests younger readers. The business section often comes next, again for primarily older readers. Almost all age groups are equally interested in science and technology, but these stories rarely make the top of the news or receive extensive coverage in the print and television media.

The public's perception of the media has changed dramatically, too. Not too long ago, the press seemed like heroes. Richard Nixon had resigned as president as a result of the news media's reports about his administration's abuse of power. Movies and television programs portrayed journalists as powerful forces for change, such as *All the President's Men,* about the *Washington Post*'s role in exposing the Watergate scandal, or as likable next-door neighbors, such as *The Mary Tyler Moore Show,* a series about a television station in Minneapolis. By the 1980s, however, the most prominent roles for journalists turned negative. In the 1981 movie, *Absence of Malice,* for example, Sally Field played a newspaper reporter who ruined the reputation of a local businessman, played by Paul Newman, by publishing erroneous articles linking him to the Mafia. In the 1987 hit *Broadcast News,* William Hurt portrayed a television reporter with blow-dried hair and a cynical view of the news, who faked a crying sequence that should have gotten him banned from the business. Instead, he moved to a bigger audience and earned more money. During Operation Desert Storm, *Saturday Night Live* ridiculed the American press corps for asking questions that would have clearly compromised the security of U.S. forces.

The credibility of journalists has clearly fallen, and not without justification. Think of today's journalist and the image that comes to mind is the swarming pack in front of a courthouse, hounding both victim and accused. But the saga doesn't stop there. In recent years, news organizations have made a stream of errors. The *Atlanta Journal-Constitution* and other news organizations identified Richard Jewell, the security guard who found the bomb during the Olympics, as a prime suspect in the attack. The report was wrong. Several Dallas news organizations reported that two Dallas Cowboy stars had been accused of raping a woman. The story also turned out to be wrong. The *San Jose Mercury News* reported that the CIA had helped Latin American drug lords ship and sell crack cocaine in low-income neighborhoods in Los Angeles—a story with many charges that under closer scrutiny the newspaper was forced to recant. There has even been downright deception. NBC's *Dateline* withheld critical information about a staged automobile test. A top *Newsweek* writer actively misled his readers about his anonymous authorship of the novel, *Primary Colors*.

Can digital journalism change the image of the media, bringing information to you that you want and will believe? There is hope. President Clinton and radio talk show host Rush Limbaugh may not agree on much. But both see the Internet as a potential positive force for news and information. Limbaugh likes the World Wide Web because it allows an individual to check the reliability of the information he or she receives from news sources, including Limbaugh's own program. "The news is available with much more detail. It's available with much more analysis. People can join chat groups and talk about the news of the day. The computer is having a profound impact on the way people are informing themselves," he says. Limbaugh checks his electronic mail constantly for information and comments from his listeners. He browses sites on sports, weather, and a variety of newspapers he would not ordinarily receive in New York, such as the *Los Angeles Times*, the *Houston Chronicle*, and the *Washington Times*. "There is a growing public distrust and distaste and skepticism about the press in general," he argues, and the Internet will provide readers and viewers with far more information that traditional news outlets provide. "It serves as a check on Peter Jennings, me, and everyone else." Fox Television President Roger Ailes perceives the Internet as a means to counter what he considers the editorial bias of many newspapers and television outlets. In many cases, you have access to the same information the reporters have. "Newspapers are biased. Television bias is obvious. The arrogance is television thinks people won't figure it out," Ailes says. "If you look at the polls on journalists, they tend to rank about the same as used car salesmen, politicians, and hookers."

But conservatives are not alone in admitting the public doesn't have much faith in the media. The *Washington Post*'s David Broder, long considered one of the most decent and thoughtful reporters in America, also sees a problem. "When the picture the people have of journalists are men and women sitting around a table arguing with each other in the loudest voices that they can muster about what the president ought to do next," he says, "or what the Congress ought to do next, then it's impossible to maintain a distinction in the public mind about what journalism is about."[17] Watergate sleuth and author Bob Woodward doesn't believe the public hates the media. But he admits, "I think that everyone is kind of confused about the information they get from the media and rightly so. I'm confused about the information I get from the media."[18]

Fewer than two out of ten Americans hold a very favorable opinion of the network television news, down from roughly three in ten only five years ago in one survey.[19] Favorable ratings for the large national newspapers such as the *New York Times* and the *Washington Post* also fell. Americans are consuming mainstream media not only less frequently these days but also with far less enthusiasm. Few people in the survey say they enjoy watching the news on television "a great deal," down dramatically from 1985. Fewer than three in ten look forward to reading the paper each day compared with more than four in ten in 1985. People who dislike network television news and daily newspapers give two main reasons: bias and emphasis on bad news. Critics claim that television carries opinion rather than fact and stoops to sensational reporting and that newspapers are inaccurate and slant stories.

That's a significant credibility gap. But it gets even worse. Nearly three of four Americans think the press actually interferes with society's ability to solve its problems. Three out of four in another poll agreed that the news media are "sensationalistic."[20] Peter Jennings, the anchor of ABC's *World News Tonight,* thinks the credibility gap may be overblown. "I am always pleased to see people come back in times of crisis," he says. "They are coming to something with a track record. At the same time on a daily basis, I am always surprised to see how many people do not recognize the difference between local television news and network television news and do not understand always that ABC *World News Tonight* and *Hard Copy* do different things." Jennings does admit, however, that there are times when the network news does slip to the lowest common denominator—a tendency he thinks established news program should resist. "When we slide toward the more populist programs, we make a serious mistake because they really do confuse the viewer. One of the instances where we did that was the O.J. Simpson trial."

Nearly forty years ago, television newsman Edward R. Murrow stood before a convention in Chicago of the Radio and Television News Directors Association. He told his colleagues that television had the ability to educate and improve society, but it now faced the prospect of becoming simply "wires and lights in a box." CBS News President Andrew Heyward recently raised a similar theme. "Why is network news losing so many viewers?"[21] he asked. The *combined* share of the three network evening news broadcasts is down more than twenty points in twenty years—from a 71 share in the 1975–76 season to a 50 share in 1995–96. And the falloff is most significant among younger viewers. Heyward allowed that the networks face increased competition from cable, and no story dominates the news such as Vietnam or Watergate. But he points his finger squarely at network news for committing what he described as "Seven Daily Sins."

The First Daily Sin is imitation. "How can the network evening news programs be so *similar*?" the CBS leader asked. "We're in a commercial, highly competitive struggle for viewers, and yet our solution for standing out in the marketplace is—do just what the competition is doing." CBS research shows that half the viewers of any given evening news broadcast—on CBS, NBC, or ABC—only watch that particular program *one night a week*. The implication is obvious: To these viewers, it doesn't make much of a difference which one they watch—or whether they watch at all.

The Second Daily Sin is predictability. "How often are you *surprised* by something you see on the news?" Heyward asked.

The Third Daily Sin is artificiality. "If you stop and really listen to how a typical television reporter tells a story, you'll hear how artificial it sounds," he said. "Even *words*—'pontiff' comes quickly to mind—that you never hear in real life. Nobody talks that way—except for us."

The Fourth Daily Sin is laziness. "The people I work with put in long hours and are very devoted to their jobs. They're certainly not lazy in the conventional sense. But I think we've all become lazy in our thinking, in our reluctance to dig out original stories and come up with new ways to tell them."

The Fifth Daily Sin is oversimplification. "Our audience is smarter and more thoughtful than a lot of us think," Heyward observed. "The people out there in America know that life is not as simple as what they see on the news: a world of heroes and villains, winners and losers, exploiters and victims. Yet that's what we show them, night after night."

The Sixth Daily Sin is hype. "Can you remember the last 'story you'll never forget?' How about the one before that? I can't," Heyward continued. "Over the years we've exaggerated so much that we've eroded our own ability to convey what's truly significant."

The Seventh Daily Sin is cynicism. "I think we're cynical about the audience and cynical about our ability to make a difference in peoples' lives," he said. "Journalists today are held in low esteem, but that doesn't have to be. Our viewers and listeners are also hungry for honest information, for help in coping with a bewildering world. We have an enormous opportunity to win our good name back—and insure our own survival in the bargain."

Without question, the media have committed a variety of sins, leading the American public to view the media with outright scorn and disbelief. But digital journalism does provide an opportunity to bridge the gap between the providers and the users of news and information. First, the new medium gives the user an opportunity to look over the shoulder of the journalist by viewing all the documents involved in a story. Second, the user can send a missive to any reporter via electronic mail, forcing journalists to listen to their public. Third, if readers and viewers don't like or trust their hometown news outlets, they can simply choose from a vast array of sources of news and information from throughout the country.

chapter three

The Movers and Shakers in Digital Journalism

In the real world, the right thing never happens in the right place and the right time. It is the job of journalists and historians to make it appear that it has.

—Mark Twain

Not so long ago, Bill Gates and Microsoft meant software and big money; now Gates has become one of the most influential media owners in the world. Steve Case, the chief executive officer of American Online (AOL), turned his marketing talent from pizzas to cyberspace. Together or individually, these two men may determine the future of the news and information we receive.

Craig Kanarick studied philosophy and computer science at the University of Pennsylvania and describes himself as a "Jewish kid from Minneapolis who ended up in New York City." At the age of nine, Elizabeth Osder became the first girl in the United States to play little league baseball when she played second base for the Englewood Orioles in New Jersey. Tom Phillips played hardball in New York and then turned toward long-distance running and frisbie outside of Seattle. Leah Gentry started playing with her father's computer when she was a kid in a small town in northern Illinois. Tom Cekay grew up on Prairie Street in Mundelein, Illinois, where the prairies actually started just west of town. Dick Duncan is an eminence gris of Time Warner. All are at the top of their game. Craig has developed Web sites for some of the most important companies on the Fortune 500. Elizabeth created the Web sites for the Rock and Roll Hall of Fame in Cleveland and the *New York Times*. Phillips is back playing hardball in New York at ABC. Leah has developed on-line newspapers in California and Illinois. Tom is the nouveau gatekeeper of the *Chi-*

cago Tribune. Dick is promoting another innovation to deliver the Internet via cable television. Here's a look at the movers and shakers in the world of digital news and information.

Bill Gates: Newsman

In 1994, Microsoft guru Bill Gates did not have a television in his office. He had virtually no interest in the Internet. Gates saw his company's future in software; that had made him the wealthiest man in America, so why change? But Bill Gates is not content with his past accomplishments. He is a student of Henry Ford, the creator of the assembly line for automobiles and one of the most innovative minds in American industry. Gates views Ford as a failure because he lost the competitive battle with General Motors. Gates does not want the same to happen to him.[1]

Today, Microsoft is a major media enterprise. Gates realized his mistake and moved quickly to correct it. Gates formed an alliance with NBC for a twenty-four-hour television news channel, MSNBC, and a World Wide Web news service of the same name. Gates lured prominent editor Michael Kinsley to Microsoft headquarters from his pundit's perch in Washington, D.C., to create the on-line magazine, *Slate.* Microsoft's *Sidewalk,* an on-line service that offers information from rock concerts to restaurant reviews, plans to lure readers and viewers away from local news papers and television stations in a variety of cities throughout the world. Microsoft Network has contracts with some of Hollywood's top creative talent to provide information and entertainment on the World Wide Web. So now when Bill Gates speaks about the news business and the Internet, people listen. Here are some of his most recent predictions:[2]

> A backlash against the Internet will develop in the press because many wild promises that have been made about the World Wide Web won't be fulfilled in the near future.

People will scour the Internet for security and privacy problems and find a small number that will be heavily touted. The scrutiny and publicity will be healthy because they'll encourage safeguards and policy debates.

Advertising revenue on the Internet will soar but not as high as some expect.

Despite these setbacks, the Internet will continue to grow in importance.

34   Gates further predicts that the distinction between communications networks will end. A single connection coming into your home or office will deliver phone, videophone, Internet, and television service. "A few years ago, some people speculated that televisions would be the primary devices people would use to interact with information on the 'information highway' of the future. The rise of the Internet has made it clear that personal computers will fill this role, instead," he says.[3]

Many people fear Gates. He is the geek almost everyone loves to hate. A prominent technology magazine, *Boardwatch*, portrayed the Microsoft leader as "Billgatus of Borg," who intended to mold the world into a single Microsoft cyborg society with one mind. Consider a joke that circulates on the Internet from time to time to underscore the attitude toward Gates: Bill Gates dies and runs into St. Peter.

"I'm not sure whether to send you to Heaven or to Hell. After all, you helped society enormously by putting a computer in almost every home in America. Yet you also created that ghastly Windows 95. I'm going to do something I've never done before. In your case, I'm going to let you decide where you want to go."

So Bill went to Hell first. It was a beautiful, clean sandy beach with clear waters and lots of bikini-clad women running around, playing in the water, laughing, and frolicking about. In Heaven,

Gates found angels drifting about, playing harps, and singing. Bill thought Hell was a better place to hang out.

Two weeks later, St. Peter found Bill, shackled to a wall, screaming among hot flames in dark caves, and being tortured by demons.

"How's everything going?" St. Peter asked.

"This is awful. This is nothing like the Hell I visited two weeks ago," Gates complained.

"That was the demo," replied Saint Peter.

35

Gates comes from a prominent Seattle family. He attended Harvard for two unsatisfying years until his high school friend, Paul Allen, saw a magazine about the first personal computer in 1975. Shortly thereafter, the friends opened Microsoft.[4] At Microsoft Gates sets a high standard. He often chides employees he thinks do not do their homework. Gates doesn't manage Microsoft by himself. He relies on an inner circle of lieutenants. Some are homegrown; others are hired guns who have brought experience and perspective from outside the company.

Does Microsoft play fair? No, of course not. It is known throughout the industry—and has been cited by the Justice Department—for its unethical and sometimes illegal behavior. But that doesn't matter. Microsoft owns the operating system that runs the world's computers. That's an advantage that the great robber barons of the nineteenth century could only dream about.[5] Chief executive officer Scott McNealy of Sun Microsystems and one of Microsoft's harshest critics argues: "I'm the world's biggest advocate of free markets and open competition. But when someone achieves a monopoly in a particular market, it is no longer a free market but a controlled economy."

Gates predicts Microsoft will double in size to nearly $10 billion in sales over the next four years. He sees no reason Microsoft can't grow one day into a $20 billion company. What drives him?

Among other things, fear. "When your sales slow down, it's probably because of some horrible mistake you made a couple of years ago. By the time your sales go down, you're dead, because it's too late to do anything about it."[6]

Fear often motivates his competitors, particularly now that he has entered the media business. At an April 1997 convention of newspaper editors in Chicago, Gates tried to convince his fellow publishers not to be paranoid about Microsoft's on-line ventures.[7] In introducing Gates to the 1,200 newspaper heavyweights, Arthur O. Sulzberger, the former publisher of the *New York Times*, described Gates as rich, smart, and powerful. Sulzberger said he asked his new media expert how he should approach the introduction of Gates. "Approach with all due humility. He may be our gate to the consumer in 10 years. No thoughts. No stories. Just fear," the publisher said his expert replied via electronic mail. A low, halting laughter came from audience, indicative of the fact that that's how most people in the news business feel toward Gates. "For better or for worse, he is also now a colleague of ours in the news business," Sulzberger said. "Microsoft competes against almost everyone in this room for reader's time and advertiser dollars. And if you don't consider it a competitor today in this increasingly digital world in which we all live, all I can say is just wait."

Gates attempted to calm the editors' fears by describing Microsoft software as the "building blocks" for newspapers to remain competitive in the digital age. "We're very interested in working with leaders in the industry to show the way technology can be applied," he said. In a testy exchange, Bob Ingle, Knight-Ridder's vice president of new media, charged that Microsoft was already luring away newspaper reporters for its city entertainment guide, *Sidewalk*. From the dais, Gates denied the charge. A show of hands around the room found that most of the newspaper executives saw Microsoft as a new and important competitor in the news business. It seemed clear that Gates's presence in the media marketplace provokes more fear than calm.

Steve Case: Marketing Maven

At 7 A.M. on August 7, 1996, Steve Case tried to log on to his company, America Online, from his home in McLean, Virginia, as he did every day to check his electronic mail: "The system is temporarily unavailable. Please try again in 45 minutes."[8] He read the same message that millions of other users received. AOL shuts down for maintenance occasionally, but Case was concerned. He made some telephone calls and then jumped into his Infinity J30 and drove to the AOL technical center in nearby Reston, Virginia. Case spoke with the company's technical guru, who told him the system had been undergoing routine maintenance. When the engineers tried to bring the system on-line, something had gone wrong with software that controls telephone calls from the main computer systems. "It was like a scene out of the control room in the movie Apollo 13," Case recalls as he watched the engineers work for an hour or so. It took nineteen hours to get the system working again, leaving millions of customers worldwide without service. The outage also affected major media operations, including the *Chicago Tribune*, the *New York Times*, and Marvel Comics, which publish on-line versions on AOL. "It made us look like a bunch of idiots," Case admits.[9]

Up until 1996, AOL was a marketing masterpiece, and Case its marketing genius. One of four children from a middle-class family in Hawaii, Case headed to the mainland for Williams College in Massachusetts. After graduating in 1980, Case began honing his marketing skills at Procter & Gamble, the home products giant in Cincinnati. He spent two years pushing hair-care products such as Abound hair-conditioning towelettes. The slogan: "Towelette? You bet!"

Case was miserable. "Managing a mature business is not my thing," he admits.[10] He then left for Pizza Hut, where he dabbled in new toppings. But he also became interested in computer technology. Two years later, he joined Quantum Computer Services, an on-line service that ultimately evolved into America Online in 1985. Case took America Online public in 1991. The next year he became chief executive officer. Like any good marketing man, he focused on expanding AOL's market share, spending heavily to pass the company's biggest competitors. To increase content and make its service more attractive, AOL signed deals with several media companies such as Knight-Ridder newspapers, Time Warner, and CNN. By the end of 1994, AOL had more than one million subscribers. By the beginning of 1996, the company had more than five million users and was adding almost 235,000 new customers a month.

Today, America Online is the world's largest and fastest-growing provider of on-line services in more than 800 cities across the United States and Europe. AOL is technically not part of the Internet; it provides *access* to the Internet and the World Wide Web. One out of every three Internet users is an AOL member. The company handles more than eleven million e-mail messages a day, hosts 7,000 chat rooms a night, and features more than 1,100 content sites. Members can access a variety of information and services, including e-mail, electronic magazines and newspapers, stock quotes, chat groups, and on-line travel services. The sites include special services only for children so parents don't have to worry that junior is downloading porno flicks; investor services such as Motley Fool, a popular investment counselor; and entertainment services from cooking to comedy. You can even buy and send flowers or a greeting card to someone online.

Case sees the company as competing with television, and AOL's management insists that *Seinfeld* and other shows are the main rivals. "It's not a choice between AOL and the Internet," Case insists.[11] "AOL is the Internet and a whole lot more." But 1996 and 1997 were not good years for AOL. Just before the August blackout, William Razzouk, president and chief operating officer of AOL, stepped down from his post after serving only four months. When Razzouk, a highly regarded former Federal Express executive, joined AOL, Case praised him as "just what the doctor ordered" to help the company's effort to turn its online offerings into a mass-market consumer medium. However Razzouk wanted to impose tight financial controls and improve customer services, and his approach did not mesh with Case's freewheeling style. After Razzouk's departure, Case decided to change the way AOL charged customers. The company was not prepared for the onslaught. By changing the monthly price from $9.95 for five hours to $19.95 for unlimited use, AOL heard from its customers, state attorneys general, and the Federal Trade Commission that the company could not simply change the payment plan without giving users a choice. On December 1, 1996, the first day of the new pricing scheme, usage surged 20 percent. Users clogged AOL lines, sending the company scrambling to add capacity to handle the increase. Some people stayed on line twenty-four hours a day once they got a connection. Others could not get on line.

As it became more and more difficult to reach AOL, the company became known as "America Off Line." Author Anne Lamott has called the company the "Agent of Lucifer." She wrote in *Salon* that "my new enemy is AOL. God, I hate AOL. AOL is the bane of my existence."[12] AOL came already installed in the computer Lamott bought for writing, and a friend convinced her to sign on to the Internet service. When the author had trouble, she called the AOL technical support line. "I only had to wait 20 minutes or so to talk to an actual human voice, which is not bad. I've called them before with little e-mail issues, and been kept waiting for entire seasons." Her Uncle Millard tried for three hours to get some new software installed. He finally got the AOL Web browser to work. "Artwork starts flooding in, and it floods and it floods and new windows keep opening and more artwork floods on and it floods away like Old Man River," she wrote. "Breathlessly, I click on Internet Connection. And guess what? More goddamn fucking artwork starts scrolling on. . . . What keeps me going is that in one moment, it's going to stop, and I will be able to type in the words '*Salon* magazine' and see my column on the computer." Alas, the screen then reads, "The server may be busy or there may be a network outage."

40

Craig Kanarick: Razorfish

Craig is a nouveau geek who found his niche in digital media after receiving a graduate degree at the Massachusetts Institute of Technology. His brown hair, pulled back in a ponytail, seems appropriate for the Greenwich Village of thirty years ago. His brown shirt matches neither his wool tie—orange with some sort of blue stripe—nor his black pants. His eyeglasses must have failed every designer testing system.

For many years, Soho (which means "south of Houston Street, pronounced only in New York as "HOW-ston" rather than the name of the Texas city), served as an artists' mecca. Today, it is the hub of what has become known as Silicon Alley, where designers for the Internet and the World Wide Web have replaced many of those who worked with paints and canvas. Kanarick is one of the top guns. He jokes about many clients who arrive at the door of on-line producers, such as the guy who comes into Razorfish and says, "I need a Web Site for my company."

"Why do you want a Web site?" Kanarick asks.

The client responds, "Because all of my major competitors have a Web Site."

"That answer isn't good enough," Kanarick replies.

The next day the client comes back and says, " I want a Web site. I've got a good reason. I was on the golf course, and I was the only executive on the golf course who didn't have a Web site."

"Not good enough," Kanarick responds.

So the client comes back and says, "I give up. You tell me what can a Web site do for me and my company?"

Kanarick and his associates decide what Razorfish can do depending on how the client responds to a variety of strategies:

41

The client can advertise a product to a new audience.

The client can launch a product internationally for a relatively low cost.

The client can reposition a product.

The client can make new product announcements.

The client can strengthen the loyalty of current customers.

The client can strengthen customer service and save money by using electronic mail rather than telephone operators.

The client could create an on-line contest to market a product.

The client could do research about customers and ask them questions about demographics.

The client could sell a product via the Internet.

After hearing the descriptions, Kanarick finds the client usually says, "Yeah, that's what I want." That's when Kanarick's team goes to work.

Razorfish clients include the most sophisticated in the Internet business such as AOL, Time Warner, and Simon & Schuster. Why should Simon & Schuster, a major publisher of paper products with 11,000 books on its booklist, turn to an electronic medium? For Simon & Schuster, the idea was simple. In the publishing business, readers recognize authors and book titles, not publishers, and Simon & Schuster wanted to develop a site to attract readers. The publishing page took six months to create—an unusually long time in the Internet business. The initial designs often are only done on paper, and it took fifteen different designs for the Simon & Schuster site. "It's like building a house. Part of it is 'how big?' Part of it is 'how complex?' Part of it is 'how good of a job?'" Kanarick explains. Razorfish designed the site for Simon & Schuster in steps.

1. The site needed to be a place where people returned frequently. Was the site going to center on information, educational, or entertainment?
2. What's the user going to do on the site? Read, search a catalogue, or talk with other people?
3. How would users get from one place to another?
4. What would users get from the Simon & Schuster page?

"It would be easy to go and buy the *New York Times* book reviews. What we've done is let anyone who reaches the site to do his or her own review. And while I don't know these people, after a while, consensus does get built." The team created reading groups around a variety of topics, including fiction, international authors, sociology, pop culture, and more.

"The cool thing is they are not bound by geography. If you wanted to start a communist propaganda reading group and couldn't find anyone in your hometown, you could find enough people nationwide or worldwide. We're using the power of technology to empower individuals to cross physical barriers," Kanarick says. In addition, there are boutiques—categories of books of special interests such as books on tape, Star Trek, and the "geek boutique" for computer aficionados. The site includes a calendar of author appearances, a "hot books" site, and an entire catalogue of 11,000 books with biographical information about the authors. "It's been one of our most challenging sites," Kanarick recalls, primarily because there was little room for error. "You can make up a stupid quiz about Argentina for some game site, and get something wrong and not many people care. You get John Grisham's bio wrong, people care."

Elizabeth Osder: The *New York Times* on the Web

It's been a bad week for Elizabeth Osder. Someone stole her collection of baseball cards from her Manhattan apartment, including an entire set of the 1957 Brooklyn Dodgers. Ironically, Osder's baseball skill as the first girl to play in the little leagues helped push her into the media. When a *New York Daily News* photographer took a picture of her one day on the field and she saw the photo in the newspaper, Osder became fascinated with the process of how that image could be transmitted and published in such a short period of time. Osder studied photography and then bumped into a friend who introduced her to the World Wide Web. Her creative juices started flowing. Since then, Osder has produced some of the finest information sites on the Web. One of her best-known products, Rockhall, is the *Cleveland Plain Dealer* site for the Rock and Roll Hall of Fame, which has attracted millions of viewers. Her most entertaining design may well be The Yuckiest Site on the Web, a children's educational project produced for *New Jersey Online*. Now she's helping create the *New York Times on the Web*.

Osder does not exactly fit the Brooks Brothers, buttoned-down atmosphere at the *Times*. She often sneaks into the conference room to toss around a baseball with an intern. "Most people sneak in there to smoke. I sneak in to play catch," she admits. Osder sees new media as being in their infancy and keeps reminding people of that. "In new media, you have to walk before you can run. You have to crawl before you can walk. We are not in a running mode. We are not erect *Homo sapiens* yet in new media. We're crawling around. So why don't we crawl elegantly?" Her central focus with the *Times*—as it has been on other projects—is the reader. "The reader is in the driver's seat," she impresses on her colleagues. "I believe that being inconsiderate to the user is the worst error." Her design revolves around the amount, or depth, of content. A printed newspaper has specific limits on the number of words and pages. You simply can't print any more. A Web site, however, can literally offer thousands of documents. Osder has a motto: "Keep it really simple. Keep it elegant. Keep it well written. Keep people moving through it." A reader can get as little as he or she wants such as a headline to as much as he or she wants, such as the original documents of a court decision.

"Right now people are surfing all over the place. They're not staying anywhere. We want people to hang out. We want them to sit in a comfortable arm chair and give them cigars and talk about the news. We don't want them to talk to us about the news. We want them to talk to one another."

Osder's first order of business has been to convince her bosses and the newspaper industry about the financial necessity of on-line publications for survival. "Every paper is going to have to go through an evolutionary process, and the industry is going to have to learn from the experience of the small and the large and find its way in the darkness," she says. "If the railroad industry had seen itself in the transportation business, it might be around today. Clearly, newspapers have to think of themselves as being in the information business, and they have to think about doing that in intelligent ways."

What exactly is the audience for on-line publications? "More people will come to the Internet as the Internet becomes easier to use, and there are more useful things on the Internet. Right now people are there for the fascination. They are only going to stay there for the utility. And that means it's easier for me to go the Internet than the yellow pages. It's easier for me to go to the

Internet to find a recipe that ran in a back issue of the *New York Times.*" Osder insists that reporters, editors, programmers, graphic artists, and everyone else involved in the process sit down to discuss how a project should be developed. That runs counter to most newspaper cultures. "Newspapers are like a linear process. The editor decides to do a story, tells another editor, they talk about it a little, and assign a reporter who often was never part of the conception of the story," Osder observes.

One concern she has is that publications may not see enough immediate income from an Internet edition and pull the plug too soon. Osder jokes that HTML—the programming codes of HyperText Markup Language for on-line products—is becoming known as an acronym with another meaning: How To Manufacture Losses. She maintains that news organizations must view the initial losses as research and development into a new medium. "My big fear is that newspapers are not going to stick behind these projects because there's no tradition of research and development in the industry," Osder says. "The industry as a whole has taken it seriously. There are newspapers—small and medium newspapers—with a lot more at stake. If Microsoft is going to move into every city and spend millions of dollars, what does that mean for the local newspaper? Microsoft is going to hire the best reporters to come next door to work."

Tom Phillips: Media Guru

Just a decade ago, Tom Phillips was playing hardball in New York. As cofounder of *Spy,* Phillips uncovered the sins both large and small of the city's rich, famous, and notorious. Then in 1993, he exchanged his hardball for a game of ultimate frisbie, as played by the employees of Starwave, an Internet company based in Bellevue, Washington. Bankrolled by Microsoft cofounder Paul Allen, Starwave created innovative and lucrative Web sites, such as *SportsZone,* which covers everything you ever wanted to know about sports. *Mr. Showbiz* reports about entertainment. *Outside Online* explores the great outdoors. *Family Planet* focuses on families. Starwave also hosts the official sites for football, auto racing, and basketball.

But Phillips, who oversaw most of Starwave's creations as senior vice president, headed back to New York to help ABC and Disney leap into cyberspace news and information. "We can't replace Peter Jennings because people still want the comfort of that image and that voice," Phillips says. Neither can cyberspace replace the editorial quality of the *New York Times*, he adds. "We can't do video as well as TV, audio as well as radio, or images as well as magazines."

But the strength of digital journalism, he argues, is the ability to integrate various media. The World Wide Web can provide news stories, photographs, audio, and video. "This medium does a reasonable job at everything," he says. In addition, the Web can provide data that are searchable and immediately available. For example, he recalls a project about the 100 greatest films in history. The editors provided a short synopsis of the plots, the names of the directors and stars, and a list of the films. Phillips sent the editors back to the drawing board to include a searchable index so that the user could access the information more easily. Phillips sees digital news and information taking away reading time from newspapers and viewing time from television. More important, however, is that the World Wide Web can reach users at work, a place where few have access to a newspaper or a television. "We are already expanding the reach of media into the workplace in a way the media were unable to do before."

Leah Gentry: The *Los Angeles Times*

It is not a good idea to underestimate Leah Gentry's intelligence. Once, a Chicago taxi driver thought she was a tourist and took her on a circuitous route to her destination; she tossed $11 at the driver, including a dime tip, proceeded to curse him out, and reported him to the police. Few underestimate her talents when it comes to digital journalism.

At the *Orange County Register*, she helped create what has been called "the newspaper without walls." Instead of a hierarchical structure that starts with the publisher at the top and goes step by rigid step down to the lowliest member of the newsroom, teams work with editors—known as "leaders"—and reporters. That approach helped earn the *Register* a Pulitzer prize for its investigation of a fertility clinic at the University of California at Irvine.

But digital journalism was Gentry's true fascination, and in the early 1990s she started dabbling in computers at the *Register*. Gentry oversaw what's known as a "bulletin board service," an electronic discussion group and chat room, where people could share information. In May 1995 Gentry surveyed on-line newspapers. She discovered that "all the Web sites were just putting up newspaper stories." As a result, she reviewed the historical development of various media. Newspapers evolved into vehicles to tell stories, but it took a long time. Radio news started with announcers reading newspaper articles over the airwaves. Television started by doing radio plays. Then each medium developed its own strengths. Gentry wrote a list about the World Wide Web and what important qualities should be brought to the new medium:

Immediacy. "You don't have to wait six hours before the presses start to run."

Interactivity. "You can actually understand who your readers are."

Multimedia. "You can provide a variety of ways to understand the news."

Technology. "No technology for technology's sake."

Making money I. "The Internet has to become a commercial enterprise and has to survive as a commercial enterprise."

Making money II. "News I want you to see you get for free," she says. You get the city budget for free. "News you want will cost you money." If you want to know Michael Jordan's free throw percentage in the past two years, it will cost you.

Gentry's passion is what she calls "nonlinear story telling." What kind of journalist will make it in this brave new world? The year 2000 conjures up an image of a cross between Buck Rogers, Bob Woodward, and Bill Gates. "Buckbobbill is a geek of the first order, who each day intrepidly climbs aboard his spaceship, jets off to probe the inner workings of the high command at Galactic Central, and writes it up in HTML to file it via e-mail," Gentry says.[13] "They (journalists) see his coming as either the downfall of the free press or the heaven-sent salvation of a dying medium."

Gentry rejects this paradigm and insists that journalists must embrace traditional news values. "The myth of the new media geek, who has no formal print experience and who writes computer code in his sleep, scares off many who would otherwise aggressively pursue an exciting new journalistic forum. If you examine the evolution of journalistic mediums, then the Web becomes a much less scary place. It took a while for radio and TV journalists to discover how to use the strengths of their particular media to tell stories. On the Web, we have that same challenge."

What is nonlinear storytelling? On the World Wide Web, you have the ability to link from one computer page location to another. Sometimes, stories must be broken into their component parts. Sometimes, the same story must be told from several points of view. That means the reporter may provide a smorgasbord of viewing options. "Journalists who succeed in 2000 will do solid reporting, careful editing, compelling writing, and visual story-telling, using the latest tools available. They'll tell their stories in whatever medium people use. But the tenets of the industry will remain the same."

Tom Cekay: The *Chicago Tribune* Digital City

For the past twenty years, Tom Cekay has been what's known as a "gatekeeper." That means Cekay is an editor who determines what gets through the "gate" into the newspaper for the reader to see. For years, the gatekeeper has been one of the most powerful people in the media, highlighting particular stories, promoting trends, sorting the journalistic wheat from the chaff—and, some would argue, restricting the flow of information. The role of gatekeeper fits Cekay, a trim, gray-haired editor with years of experience. Will that role change in the digital age? "The traditional role of the editor stays the same. Do the readers need to see this? Is it intelligently done? Is it sophisticated reporting? Is it what the newspaper wants? So, in many respects, the role of the editor is very much the same as the printed edition," says Cekay, who has worked for newspapers in Oregon, Ohio, and Illinois.

The original research on journalistic gatekeepers began in 1949 when David Manning White of Boston University persuaded a small city news editor to keep all of the copy from the Associated Press, United Press, and the International News Service from a one-week period. The editor, who was given the name "Mr. Gates," agreed to provide written explanations why he had selected or rejected items from the newspaper. About one-third of the time, Gates rejected stories because he did not think the story was true. Two-thirds of the time, the editor rejected stories because he lacked sufficient space in the newspaper, or he had already chosen a similar story for publication.[14] The editor did allow that he had a few personal opinions that could influence his decisions. "I have few prejudices, built-in or otherwise, and there is little I can do about them. I dislike Truman's economics, daylight saving time, and warm beer, but I go ahead using stories on them and other matters if I feel there is nothing more important to give space to. I am also prejudiced against a publicity-seeking minority with headquarters in Rome (Roman Catholics), and I don't help them a lot. As far as preferences are concerned, I go for human interest stories in a big way. My other preferences are for stories well-wrapped up and tailored to suit our needs."[15] In 1966, a second study showed that Mr. Gates made roughly the same decisions. He used fewer human interest stories in 1966 than in 1949, but the editor chose more international stories. Asked for his definition of news, Mr. Gates replied, "News is the day by day report of events and personalities and comes in variety which should be presented as much as possible in variety for a balanced diet."[16]

Researchers found a set of factors that often determine what news gets into the media. Cekay finds some, but not all, of the gatekeeper's role applicable to digital journalism:

> *Time span.* Events that coincide within the time frame of publication are more likely to pass through media gates. "I've never thought about it in those terms," he says, particularly now that digital journalism allows constant updates.
>
> *Intensity of threshold value.* Events are more likely to pass through the media gates if they are of great magnitude or if they have recently increased in magnitude. "That's one thing we do very well. When it's a major breaking story, this is a perfect medium to put out a lot of information. I think people do turn to our site, such as the TWA 800 crash and the Olympic bombing," Cekay says.
>
> *Clarity or lack of ambiguity.* Events with some sort of final outcome are likely to pass through media gates. Cekay thinks this tenet does

not play a crucial role in digital or traditional journalism. "I think that there are few things that are that clear-cut that we cover in the news business."

Cultural proximity or relevance. The media are most likely to accept news events that have close cultural relevance for the audience. "I want to be very careful about creating a self-fulfilling prophecy where we are saying what the people say they want and in doing so we become an exclusive site that is not for the public at large. I want to make sure we're not narrowcasting. I want to make certain my mother is interested in what we put on this site, and my little boy is interested in what we put on this site, and I want to make sure my neighbor does, and the guy on the other side of the state who's a farmer."

51

Consonance or unexpectedness. Expected events, such as a school board passing a budget, are likely to pass through the media gates. Unexpected events such as a hijacking of an airplane also are likely to receive prominent play. "I am much more interested in the unexpected," Cekay says.

Continuity. If an event or news story passes through the media gate once, it probably will pass through the gate again. Cekay agrees. "That's why it's important to think about what you do the first time."

Composition. Because gatekeepers look at the day's news in its entirety, some items get selected merely because they contrast with others. "I don't really worry about that," he observes.

Sociocultural values. Values of both the gatekeepers and their readership can also influence selection beyond the other factors.[17] "I think news judgment is affected because you appreciate the importance of a story. If you had a serious illness, you realize how people are affected by it. If you're twenty-four, you may not appreciate that people have to deal with things like that. If it's model rocketry, you know there are people out there who care about model rocketry. Otherwise, you're taking your intelligence out of the mix."

So far, digital journalism has not developed its own rules and procedures, Cekay says, simply because it's too young. "I think the instincts we follow are the instincts we learned at the newspaper. I think we are very close to following those patterns, which are tried and true and lead to a good package and a report. But it's clear to me that as we grow with this, we're going to have to stretch that model because we're dealing with a lot more. This is just the infancy of this medium. Right now, we're taking the old formula how do they do it in newspapers, how do they do it in radio, and how do they do it in television."

One significant advantage of this new medium is the ability to let the reader into the process. "We can come up with conclusions on what we see and intelligently report that to you," Cekay says. "What's even better is we can say we're so sure that we are interpreting the news in a fair, unbiased, and proper way that we feel confident that we will give you all the documentation and you can check us. You can see for yourself."

Richard Duncan: Time Warner's RoadRunner

Richard Duncan is definitely not a computer geek. Even though Time Warner encourages a more relaxed dress code on Fridays, Duncan still wears a gray suit and white shirt. He forgoes a tie this Friday, but one is almost certainly nearby. For more than thirty years, Duncan has held some of the most important positions at *Time*, including chief of correspondents, in which capacity he coordinated the magazine's worldwide news coverage. He admits that he's really a "print guy" at heart and gets his news every morning by turning on the television and reading the *New York Times*. It's sort of a habit, he allows, after so many years at *Time*.

Only one of his four children uses the Internet. His fifteen-year-old son gets information about fishing and baseball games from the computer. "We're not exactly an Internet family," he admits. But, if you want to get Duncan excited, just ask him about

RoadRunner, the Internet program he heads—yes, that's RoadRunner, the Warner Brothers' cartoon character that outwits Wiley Coyote.

What's so special about RoadRunner, the information service? In Ohio, California, New York, Maine, Florida, and Hawaii, subscribers to the Time Warner cable system can use the same cable to enter the Internet. That process allows a home computer to get information from Time Warner's Pathfinder Web site and the Internet at speeds far faster than a typical home modem. "The world is fed up with the speed problem on the Internet. We learned people want news. News is the single most popular thing that is devoured," Duncan says. "People want to be stimulated."

RoadRunner offers a potpourri of news and information. The news services include Reuters; nearly twenty Time Warner print publications, such as *Time*, *People*, *Sports Illustrated*, and *Fortune*; and local newspaper reports. The service provides tips on subjects from gardening to personal finance, and information from movie reviews to anatomy lessons with a variety of links to local schools, hospitals, and libraries.

Although this potpourri retains much that's from the print media, Duncan thinks the Internet and the World Wide Web need to create their own identity. "We got print guys in the business. We got people who did television. We got the techies, and now we're starting to get the movie people in. We are sort of doing our own thing, which is an extension of where we came from. But we are not really assimilating the other people's techniques really well," he acknowledges.

Still, Duncan sees several positive trends, including the ability of users to talk back to journalists. "Interactivity is the key. If you tell the journalist to go to hell, maybe you should get a response back," he says. Duncan would like to create a dialogue between users and journalists in an attempt to bridge the credibility gap the news business faces. During several on-line discussions with users, Duncan agreed with complaints that *Time* had made mistakes on gun stories. But he also got some National Rifle Association members to admit that their organization had put out bad statistics. "I think there's a real opportunity to develop a relationship between the user and the producer. The press brings bad news, and the press is kind of arrogant. The people yapping after the president has contributed to it. If there's a little evangelism here, maybe we can break that down interactively. I'd like to see that."

So far, white males tend to hold control over the levers of digital journalism among the major organizations. But it is not absolute. Women like Gentry of the *Los Angeles Times* and Osder of the *New York Times* are gaining a strong foothold in a variety of on-line publications. The digital powerbrokers tend to be relatively young by conventional newsroom standards, primarily because the younger one is the more likely that person knows how to use a computer more effectively. Although individuals can proclaim themselves reporters and put up a news site on the Web, large companies tend to dominate the information business, primarily because brand names like *Time* and the *Chicago Tribune* provide a link with journalistic integrity. That's unlikely to change any time soon in the early evolution of digital journalism.

chapter four

Immediacy, Interactivity, and Intimacy

Information is the currency of democracy.
> —Thomas Jefferson

Just before 2 A.M. on July 27, 1996, the Associated Press sent out a bulletin that a bomb had exploded at the Olympics in Atlanta. Up and down the East Coast of the United States, many newspaper readers had no idea that morning that something had happened. The problem: the story occurred after the deadlines of many newspapers. At the *New York Times*, for example, the editors decided to go with the AP story in the final edition and downplay its importance under a single-column headline. The final edition, however, reaches few readers. "The paper was uncertain at that time of the story's dimensions and wanted to be cautious," says one editor.

At the on-line edition of the *Times*, the staff also was about to publish the morning edition when the news broke. "Normally, we run basically what's in the paper at this hour, but we decided to wait a bit to include the news of the explosion as an 'update' and not use the edited wire story printed in the paper," recalls Bernard Gwertzman, senior editor of the *New York Times on the Web*. The *Times*'s on-line edition offered its own story that hit the Web at 2:30 A.M., reporting that dozens were injured. The story quoted eyewitnesses interviewed by CNN and NBC with a photo from Olympic Park. At 5:15 A.M., the FBI held a news conference in which the bombing was described as an "act of terrorism." By 6 A.M., the *Times*'s on-line story included the decision that the Olympic games would continue. In addition, *Times* photographer Bart Silverman, who was using a digital camera, sent pictures from Atlanta. Shortly after noon Saturday, the on-line edition added information from the *Times*'s reporters on the scene. "It was a good experience for the on-line paper and demonstrated the utility of the Web page when the printed paper is locked in by printing deadlines," says Gwertzman, who spent years with the printed version as a reporter and editor. Another option Gwertzman and the on-line editors learned was to wait until they all the important elements without rushing to use first reports from the scene, which proved to be overly sensational.

Immediacy, interactivity, and *intimacy:* those are the watchwords for many digital journalists. A user can have immediate information, can interact with reporters or other readers, and can create his or her own news service, "The Daily Me," a personal cross section of the news.

Immediacy

In many cases, the credibility of the content stands as the key to success, and news outlets tend to do better when they stick to what they know—generally local coverage. In eastern Washington state, for example, the Department of Energy was scheduled to announce on August 6, 1996, what company would receive a nearly $5 billion contract to operate the Hanford Nuclear Reservation. It was one of the most significant stories in the region of the decade because 13,000 local residents worked at the plant. Unfortunately for the local newspaper, the *Tri-City Herald*, the announcement was scheduled for late morning—a time when radio and television stations had a decided advantage in getting the news out first. In its lead story the day of the announcement, the *Herald* printed a box saying that it would announce details about the contract winner on its Web site as soon as the news was known.

"We did this because we knew we would get killed by broadcast, so we had nothing to lose," news editor Andy Perdue says. On the Web site, Perdue and his staff assembled dozens of background stories about the plant from the archives, as well as links to other Hanford-related Web sites. Nearly three hours before the formal announcement, the Herald got word that Fluor Daniel had won the contract and put the story up immediately on the on-line edition. The on-line edition scooped the printed edition; more important, the on-line edition beat local radio and television. "Almost immediately, the newsroom phones started ringing, and I started getting e-mail from readers who were watching the Web site for news," says Perdue. The Hanford story gave the Web site its best day, with 16,000 visits.

58

Interactivity

In Indiana, Toyota selected a site near Evansville for a $800 million truck plant. Readers wanted to know everything about the operation, says James Derk, the computer editor at the *Evansville Courier*. "They wanted to know how to get a job there, the timetable for the plant, how to get hired, how the Japanese do business," Derk says. So the newspaper devoted an entire section of its electronic newspaper to the arrival of the Toyota truck plant in nearby Princeton. The site listed job openings, information about the plant, and a guide to Japanese culture and customs. The site included news stories about the plant, such as the need to expand nearby fire stations and the possible environmental impact on one town. Toyota actually requested that the newspaper remove the manufacturer's logo from the site, Derk adds, "to make it clear that it was not an official company site. The letter said the site was 'so good' that it looked company-sponsored."

How do new media engage the body politic of today in subjects the old media consider important such as politics? "You have to invite controversy," says Elizabeth Osder, content editor of the *New York Times on the Web*. "You have to be where the discussion is happening." That's why the *Times* and National Public Radio launched an ambitious project to engage the national and local electorates in a political debate during the 1996 campaign. "You can only engage people who want to come and think and read. We can't counter the current state of American culture where people don't care about a lot," she admits. "But it's a newspaper's job to set the agenda that these are the important items of the day."

For the final six weeks of the 1996 campaign, the *Times* invited the readers of the Internet edition to "join a national dialogue about the issues." The topics included community, money, rights, safety, and international affairs with discussion groups headed by journalists and scholars. Unfortunately, some forums degenerated after a short time. "It didn't go as well as we expected. We expected that *Times*'s readers were sort of a different cut, more erudite. We thought we'd get a real dialog going, and then we got stuff like 'you suck.' 'And you suck more,' " admits one editor. "It was ridiculous. We pulled down a number of sites because of the low level of the dialog."

In another section of the on-line *Times*, you could compare the Democratic and Republican Party platforms on a variety of issues, including defense spending, trade, and foreign policy. You could even put together your personal political views and compare those with the candidates for the presidency, the U.S. Senate, and the House of Representatives on issues such as juvenile crime, the federal deficit, the economy, the family, America's global role, immigration, poverty and welfare, and race and opportunity. There was even a quiz about your knowledge of the issues facing America today. Here's one series of questions:

59

Issue No. 1:

Background: voters vote their pocketbooks, and the nation's. Bill Clinton made this abundantly clear in 1992 with his campaign mantra, "It's the economy, stupid." But this year's money issues are less clear.

Synopsis: This quiz tests your grasp of the campaign's fiscal issues and provides the answers with some context.

Question No. 1: Which is the single largest expenditure in the federal budget?

Choose one:

Defense
Welfare
Social Security
Interest payments on the debt
Medicare

The correct answer: Social Security benefits account for one-fifth of the federal budget, making it the largest single item. The $320 billion in annual payments mean a rate of spending of $15,000 per second.

Background: Lower trade barriers and cheaper labor outside the United States have driven thousands of manufacturing jobs overseas. How much do economists estimate it costs American consumers to keep a single $20,000–$30,000 a year manufacturing job in the United States?

$170,000
$70,000
$30,000
$20,000

The correct answer: It costs an average of $170,000 a year to keep a manufacturing job in the United States, according to a 1994 study by the Institute for International Economics. When companies move their plants outside the United States, where they can pay workers lower wages, that can translate into savings for consumers.

I chose "defense" and "$70,000." As a former Washington reporter and teacher of international affairs, I felt humbled by my lack of knowledge. The *Times* and NPR did provide a useful exercise in challenging us about what we think we know and what we actually know about public affairs. This approach underlines how new media can provide a unique function that other outlets cannot. I am certain I have seen a number of graphs and news articles that provided me with the information in the quiz. But I will remember the information now, far more than I would from reading a story about these issues or seeing a colorful graphic in *USA Today*. The question-and-answer format may be part of the reason. But the reason may also be that on-line information is available anytime, not only on a single day or with a single glance on a harried morning going to work.

61

The 1996 political campaign also marked the emergence of the Internet as a new medium for obtaining information about candidates. In short, it was a test run for the year 2000. About one in ten voters visited a Web site for news and information about the campaigns, while roughly the same number visited Internet sites for the candidates or political parties.[1] During the first presidential debate on October 6, 1996, anchor Dan Rather announced the address for the CBS's Web site, and within a few minutes, according to the network, more than one million people tried to log on. On election night, users jammed the Internet for news about the returns, while network television saw its ratings drop significantly from 1992. Hackers also attacked the *New York Times* on the Web, trying to take it down. While the attack slowed the *Times*'s results considerably, the on-line edition stayed up and running.

Intimacy

On-line publications are trying to strengthen ties to the community, a traditional role for most local newspapers. Steve Yelvington, managing editor of the on-line edition of the *Minneapolis Star Tribune*, is trying to determine how to create a sense of community among his users. In fact, it may be somewhat easier than with a printed newspaper because people who have left Minneapolis now have a touchstone with those in the city. Cyberspace may not recreate a crisp Minnesota morning, but there is the ability to speak with people who share a common bond or interest. "I used to live in a downtown high-rise that was as big as the entire town in which I now live, but it was not a community," Yelvington observes. "You want to know who understands community building? Pastors. Neighborhood bartenders." Volleyball leagues, coffee hours, and discussion forums all contribute to the process that transforms visitors into members of a community, Yelvington says. That's what he's trying to create on-line. "Set up an on-line environment in which users can meet, interact with one another, share their thoughts informally," he says. An on-line publication should "get people talking. Ask questions. Provoke disagreement. Seed the system with some colorful personalities. Talk about the news but also talk about coffee, stupid drivers, and religion. Add formal and informal programs. Maybe even sponsor a get-together so these virtual neighbors can meet in person. It'll work."

The death of Princess Diana underlined exactly how the Internet can provide a sense of community, in this case an outpouring of grief over the death of an individual. While newspapers and broadcast outlets chronicled the automobile crash and the funeral, the Internet allowed individuals to express their sadness and anger about what happened. Nine out of ten Americans paid some attention to the events, a survey found, while an estimated 54 percent followed the tragedy closely.[2]

On the Internet, tens of thousands of mourners from around the world gathered to obtain more information and to express their feelings by posting messages on memorial bulletin boards and taking part in chat sessions. This facet of the Internet—the ability to interact with others—underscores the principle difference between new media and traditional media. The Internet provided individuals the ability to talk about news and information actively and immediately with a wide group of people rather than passively watching the events on television. Some mourners sent virtual roses created in computer code: @----}---------. Others expressed their outrage at the photographers who followed behind the automobile and called for a boycott of tabloid newspapers in Britain. Some even speculated about a plot to kill the princess.[3]

Another significant trend is toward personalized editions on the Internet, where someone can select specific stories to read. Take the case of Brad Bartley. He is not the only student from Oklahoma at the Massachusetts Institute of Technology, but he is the only one from Quapaw. His hometown lies in the northeastern corner of Oklahoma and in the last census had a population of 985. When Bartley arrived at MIT in 1993, he was not awed by Boston. But he wanted some news from back home in Oklahoma and couldn't find much in the distinctly New England-oriented media. He got an occasional score about the football or basketball teams. He got a glimpse of the weather in Oklahoma when a local television station showed the national radar map. But Boston is Boston, and Oklahoma is not exactly on the radar screen of the Beantown media.

Bartley is a no-nonsense kind of guy who might have been cast in the film, *Oklahoma*, where Gordon MacRae sang about the winds sweeping across the plains. So Bartley decided to do something about his info-gap. He and seven other freshmen took their concerns to the MIT Media Lab. That's where Nicholas Negroponte, the author of *Being Digital*, holds court in a futuristic building constructed from an odd array of ornamental cement, white tile, and glass designed by I. M. Pei. The MIT Media Lab in Cambridge is the mecca for those who want to know what the new millennium will bring, be it the newspaper of the future, virtual reality, or any other buzzword.

Fortunately, the Media Lab's ayatollahs listen to good ideas, and Bartley and his fellow freshmen had a good one. Together with researcher Pascal Chesnais, the freshmen devised a customized, personal news service for subscribers, named *FishWrap*, which is updated instantaneously via computer. Wrapping fish is what people used old newspapers to do, and that's what this experiment was about—forcing newspapers to do more than ultimately wrap fish and line parakeet cages. Since the creation of *FishWrap*, the mainstream media from the *Wall Street Journal* to Time Warner offer dozens of variations of what the MIT freshmen conceived. The *San Francisco Examiner-Chronicle's* Internet edition, The Gate, actually uses the personalized computer structure developed at MIT, as do newspapers in Italy and Brazil.

While there are a number of variations on the personal news services, here's how the original, *FishWrap*, works: About seven hundred people subscribe to the news service. A computer program asks three questions. First, the computer needs to know your hometown, specifically the zip code. Second, the computer asks about your academic interests and your personal interests. From that profile, robot programs seek out key words, such as "computers" or "Oklahoma," to construct a daily news and information site from news stories filed into the computer's database from the Associated Press, the Boston newspapers, Knight-Ridder, *Zagat's Restaurant Guide*, and other news providers. The main page shows precisely what news sources have provided the information. You can then focus on a news category and view summaries of stories. If the summary of an article seems interesting, you can call up the full text with relevant graphics or audio. As a navigation aid at the top of each computer screen, *FishWrap* displays a bar that indicates where you are. Like its printed cousins, *FishWrap* has a front page called "Page One." In a spirit of democracy—perhaps news editors would call it anarchy—each of the *FishWrap* users actually can determine what goes on the front page. If someone thinks that the group should read a particular story, that individual can put it on the front page. These selections allow users to enjoy the breadth of community interests and forces individuals to be exposed to ideas outside of their personal experiences and choices.

When Bartley showed me how the system worked, that day's lead story dealt with the physical attack against a Turkish politician visiting Hungary. "I'd read that," says Bartley, an electrical engineering student. "It's weird enough." But if not enough people read that story, it falls down to the bottom of the front page and then off the front page after thirty-six hours. The addition of the "Page One" stories came after survey results found that students were indeed concerned about becoming isolated from events outside their parochial interests. But democracy can create some odd, but distinctive, news decisions. When the Oklahoma City bombing occurred, for example, students read another story more often—a report about the mugging of Big Bird on the same day. "The icon of your childhood getting pummeled was more important to the students," Chesnais says. "It struck a chord among students."

After the front page, an MIT subscriber can access a constant stream of stories from the Associated Press. When the bombing in Oklahoma happened, for example, Bartley turned to his computer to monitor what was happening in his home state and watched television on CNN. "Generally, I like to read more than watch television because it's more complete. It's better here on the computer because it was more restrained. I get this when I want it on the computer, and it's up-to-date," he says.

The next section of *Fishwrap* is local, national, and international news. In his case, Bartley's local news comes from Oklahoma.

Most of the time, Bartley does not find much that interests him, but he's glad to know the weather in his hometown this day is better than in often-frigid Cambridge. For his personal page, "Stuff That I Like," the MIT student has chosen computer technology, book reviews, architecture, and photo essays. Today, he gets nothing that interests him in the review section, which includes books about Fergie, Oprah Winfrey, and a reading by singer Johnny Cash. Under the photo essays, he retrieves photographs about George Gershwin and South Africa.

When Bartley finishes reading his *FishWrap*, the computer retrieves all the articles he had scanned and offers a clipping service to save the stories. After logging off, the computer will reorganize the personal edition if Bartley has changed his reading habits or added new topics to his choices. That's a key element of *Fishwrap*, to notice how you change your reading habits. For example, when advisor Chesnais's sister was in Rwanda during the 1995 massacres, he says, "*FishWrap* followed my reading habits." Chesnais started choosing more news about Rwanda, and the computer sensed he wanted more stories about the country. When his sister left Rwanda, Chesnais saw the computer program push the stories down in importance as he selected fewer of them. The customized news service at MIT, which is available only to students and faculty from the university, can offer information based on where a reader may be traveling. If someone's going to Finland, for example, the user can choose news about that country to appear before going and end after the individual returns.

FishWrap also tries to provide context for readers about stories, particularly those in developing countries. Here, for example, is a Reuters dispatch about recent floods in China:

SHANGHAI, CHINA —China fears its worst flooding disaster this century with rising waters already killing hundreds of people and devastating farms and fisheries in its eastern region. Spring rains which annually bring calamity to tens of millions have been compounded by the effects of global warming and some meteorologists predict the worst inundation in a hundred years.

After reading this story, you might say, "What a pity!" Then you would move on. Here's how *FishWrap* makes the story more relevant to users in Cambridge, providing a variety of data easily accessible on the Internet: The MIT news service pulls out the details on the worst floods in the United States. *FishWrap* points out that more than 14,000 people in Boston speak Chinese. The service creates a graphic of the area in China affected by the floods and places it on a map of Boston, showing that nearly all of the Boston suburbs would be under water if a similar flood occurred in Massachusetts. The damage of $500 million would cost every person in Boston $2,200 or about 7.5 percent of the average yearly income in the city. The number of households affected by the Chinese flood—220,000—would mean roughly all the houses in Boston.

At Individual Inc., a Boston-based news service with an estimated 400,000 readers, president and chief executive officer Michael Kolowich sees some systematic guidelines for users of personalized news services.

News consumers want filtering. "It's defensive. Make sure I don't miss anything important," he says. Newspapers generally do a relatively good job at this requirement, while radio and television do not provide enough specific information.

Finding, or the ability to search for data. One day some information may not be important, but the next month that story may be critical to a decision. Newspapers have archives, but they often are not immediately available to readers except via expensive computer databases such as Lexis-Nexis.

Browsing. "I put myself in the hands of someone else whom I trust," Kolowich says. "I trust this editor or this news organization to inform me or tell me what's important or entertain me. A gatekeeper and a guide." All media can perform this function, depending on the individual (see chapter 3).

Communing. "Put me in a community that shares an interest," Kolowich says. "Sales people almost inevitably use a general interest topic as a conversation starter," such as the weather or a news story.

68

The Internet and the personalized news service can provide each of these qualities to the user, while traditional media can provide only one or two. For example, a recent Yankelovich survey found that young adults complain that if they edited the paper it would be better organized—arranged "so you can find what you want"—and there would be "more things that are entertaining to read."

One specialized format of custom news is what's known as "real-time" reporting. As real time would indicate, the news moves rapidly via computers as quickly as information becomes known. More than a dozen news agencies—Reuters, Dow Jones, and Bloomberg—offer financial news to more than 500,000 customers in financial institutions, businesses, and government agencies through subscriptions. The agencies provide anything from government data to corporate earnings in rapid fire for subscribers to use the information, often to make business decisions and investments. A recent comparison of the news in the *Wall Street Journal* printed edition and its sister services of Dow Jones found some intriguing differences in conventional reporting and the real-time variety.[4] In a somewhat sobering research survey about what may exist in the future of on-line journalism, the authors found that real-time reporting had less explanatory information— a strong suit of many printed publications—and short stories with fewer sources. "A fast food analogy comes closer to describing the two methods, with real time being fast and traditional practices representing home cooking," the authors note. "The inevitable question arises as to which food is better—for journalism and its readers?"[5]

Other questions arise about customized news services. The services are by definition egocentric. You choose what you want to read and can filter out other information. The role of the newspaper reporter and editor—the gatekeepers of information—are limited, if not eliminated altogether, in providing the user with what is important and what is not. Users may become isolated from their neighborhood, city, state, and nation because they have filtered out any information about the global village. "Say you have a user who has set up a customization agent so that he or she gets favorite sports teams' news and selected stocks. OK, the president is assassinated. That's a gimme. You override and give them that headline regardless of stated news preferences," argues Leah Gentry of the *Los Angeles Times*. "But what about something really interesting, but not so earth-shattering, say, a hijacked jet crashing into the ocean and killing all onboard? At what point do you stop respecting the wishes of the user and start feeding them what you think is important?" Gentry is not certain what she would decide.

If a newspaper provides the option for an exclusive, personal news service, then the provider should stick by its commitment, maintains Melinda McAdams, the designer of the *Washington Post's* digital edition. "I am a user who absolutely does not want that allegedly important news flash. I will 'never' have only one source of news on my desktop or in my life, and these news flashes would surely, certainly, undoubtedly be redundant—and thus unwelcome—for me," she insists. Steve Yelvington of the *Minneapolis Star Tribune* thinks the customized services will eventually gravitate toward the community newspaper. "There's a belief that computers are changing the ground rules, but those ground rules aren't what we thought they were, and when we look closely at the World Wide Web experience, we find that computers aren't very good at handing power over to individuals anyway," he argues. "They're incredibly clumsy devices for navigating through information space. They're slow and unreliable. I think the market will demand that broad-but-shallow 'Daily We' element in any customizable environment."

What impact will these customized news products have on the future of the printed page? More than half of the cost of publishing a newspaper includes taking the words from a reporter's computer screen, printing those words on paper, and then shipping that paper product to a subscriber's home or business. While there are many jobs associated with printing and trucking the printed paper, it seems much more cost-effective and efficient to simply move the contents of a computer screen at the newspaper's office to the computer screens of the subscribers. Perhaps it's useful to go back to Brad Bartley, the MIT student who helped create the "Daily Me" and will be the user of news in the future. "I think it would probably be fine if personalized news replaced newspapers. You get it in a lot more convenient form. You get it where and when you what it. It's easier to keep it around rather than clipping it and watching it get yellow."

Bartley sees an upside for newspapers. "Costs can go down for a newspaper like maintaining a warehouse full of paper and a fleet of truck drivers. You can get the quick response time of television with the completeness of text. It will get easy to compare things by reading news from different sources side by side. It just seems like a big win situation."

Doing Digital Journalism: The *Chicago Tribune* and TWA 800

I want the *Tribune* to continue to be after I am gone as
it has been under my directions, an advocate of
political and moral progress and in all things to follow
the line of common sense.   —Joseph Medill,
                                Chicago Tribune publisher

72   Cornelia Grumman presses the sixth-floor button on the elevator at the Henry Horner public housing project. The City of Chicago has planted flowers outside the building, where gangs and drug pushers run the West Side neighborhood. The elevator does not work well and reeks of urine. After two tries, Grumman finally reaches the fifth floor and walks up one flight of stairs strewn with garbage. Two young boys climb on a safety fence that's supposed to keep them from falling into the garden below, but seems more like a cage to keep them in.

Grumman, a reporter for the *Chicago Tribune*, wants to know what people on welfare think about massive changes in the federal program. She visits twenty-four-year-old Melineice Reed and her three children who live in well-kept, but tiny, three-room apartment. Reed has lived in the projects all her life. The next day she has an interview for a job as a cleaning woman, and she's a bit nervous. "Do you have anything to wear that's nice?" Grumman asks. "Nice enough," the woman says. Down the street, a group of worshippers gathers at a Baptist church for Sunday services. Grumman finds several people willing to talk about the federal plan that would limit benefits for those on welfare. One woman, Demitraius Dykes, has spent all of her twenty-six years on welfare. A recovering drug addict, she has five children. Dykes says she's trying to turn her life around by attending a course to learn office skills. "I don't want my kids to grow up and think they should sit around and wait each month for their check," she says. Grumman scribbles notes, runs a tape recorder, and takes a picture. Although she does not like using video cameras, Grumman wishes she had one along for this interview because Dykes is a good talker.

The reporter works for the Internet edition of the *Chicago Tribune*. She is a new breed of journalist—the digital journalist—and it strikes more than a few observers that the *Chicago Tribune* is an odd leader in the digital age. Along Michigan Avenue, the Tribune Tower juts skyward like a Gothic cathedral, a monument to journalistic tradition and values. The exterior walls contain chunks of stones from the Alamo, the Taj Mahal, and even the Great Wall of China. Inside, the important doctrines of the journalist's craft are etched in the walls of the entry:

> Whoever would overthrow the liberty of a nation thus began by subduing the freeness of speech. —Benjamin Franklin

> I do not agree with a word that you say, but I will defend to the death your right to say it. —Voltaire

> An intolerant majority swayed by passion or by fear may be prone in the future as it has often been in the past to stamp as disloyal opinions with which it disagrees.
> —U.S. Supreme Court Associate Justice Louis Brandeis

Nearby, tourists gawk at the newspapers encased behind glass. The headlines include one from November 11, 1918, "Great War Ends." Another from May 22, 1927, "Lindbergh Lands in Paris." Tradition has been a watchword at the newspaper even though the company has been at the forefront of innovations—some bad and some good. One publisher instituted a series of changes because he thought English spellings were too complicated. "Through" became "thru," for example, a practice that continued into the 1970s. There have been mistakes, such as the famous headline in 1948, "Dewey Defeats Truman." For the most part, however, the *Tribune* has been a bedrock of conservatism and journalistic excellence in the Midwest.

On the fifth floor of the Tribune Tower, something not so traditional is going on. The *Tribune* is one of the few newspapers in the country that has reporters like Grumman who work exclusively for the Internet edition. The reporters write stories, take pictures, operate video cameras, and create digital pages to produce one of the most innovative on-line editions available today.

The *Tribune* is one of more than 1,000 commercial on-line publications in the United States.[1] Of these publications, four out of ten concentrate on subjects such as business. Three out of ten deliver a full range of news on a daily basis. One in ten is a nondaily publication, and about the same number offer only limited services, meaning that the publications update stories less frequently than the printed newspapers or provide a limited range of stories. Fewer than one in ten are promotional sites with no regularly updated news.

At the *Tribune,* computer consultant Leah Gentry forged the design of the on-line edition. She intended to deliver to users what she thought they should have and what they want. She proudly calls the team "the hardest working band in the business." Gentry is the band leader and has a set of exacting standards that would make any conductor envious. She calls them "Leah's Rules": All the regular rules of journalism apply. Reporting and editing must be solid. Facts must be checked and rechecked. If you're going to use this week's gizmo, it has to help advance the telling of the story in a meaningful way. No instant publishing; everybody has his or her finger on the press, but nobody is allowed to post a page that hasn't gone through the editing process. Reporters need to think of the medium while reporting. In addition to story information, they must gather or assign information for animated or still graphics, video, and audio. "The main rule: what we're doing is journalism, not stupid technology tricks," she says.

The *Tribune* Internet edition, which debuted in March 1996, contains most of the information from the print version—news, sports, job listings, real estate and automobile advertisements, weather, stocks, and television listings. For its readers, the Internet edition offers in-depth stories, special technology reports, games, discussion groups, and everything someone would ever want to know about the Chicago Bears and the Chicago Bulls. The Internet edition also provides audio interviews and information from the company's radio station and video from the Tribune's twenty-four-hour-a-day news service, Chicagoland Television.

The Internet band includes Tom Cekay, a former financial editor of the *Tribune*. He is the editorial controller—the gatekeeper of what makes it on-line and what does not. "The differences are that the demands on the editor are much higher because the editor has to know a lot more stuff than on the paper. The editor has to know about the audio that goes into these packages. The editor has to know about the video that goes into these packages," he says. He admits that he has to edit "a whole lot faster" because of the constant deadline pressure of the up-to-the-minute Internet edition. That can mean mistakes can creep into copy, but it's much easier to correct the errors easily and quickly an option rarely available to the printed edition.

The rest of the band is young, energetic, and sometimes irreverent. The newspaper editors and reporters at the *Tribune* tend toward blue shirts, khaki pants, and expensive shoes. With few exceptions, this band tends toward T-shirts, blue jeans, and tennis shoes. By far the best-dressed in her business suits, Grumman studied public policy at Duke University and the Kennedy School of Government at Harvard. She worked as a freelance reporter in China and booked rock and roll bands there, too. Another reporter, Darnell Little, studied computer programming and developed telephone software for Bell Labs before becoming a journalist. Stephen Henderson wrote editorials for newspapers in Lexington, Kentucky, and Detroit before joining the *Tribune*'s Internet staff.

During the 1996 Democratic convention in Chicago, the Internet edition of the newspaper reached nearly 100,000 users a day—more than most newspapers in the nation. Reporter Little conceived a historical tour of some of the twenty-five previous political conventions in the city, starting with the one that nominated Abraham Lincoln in 1860. Little, who received both a master's degree in engineering and journalism from Northwestern, went to the Chicago Historical Society to get a visual sense of how to conduct a tour on the World Wide Web. "The idea was to take people on a tour that was a virtual museum," he explains. There were three parallel streams: A tour through six of the conventions, a behind-the-scenes look at what was happening in Chicago at the time, and archives and political cartoons from the various eras. "The reporting is the same as working for a standard newspaper—gathering the information and talking to people. But you put it together and write it differently."

Before writing the story, Little designs a series of storyboards for what each of the main pages will show, a practice used extensively in the film, television, and advertising industries. The storyboard contains an outline of a page's content, graphics, and computer links to other stories. After Little reports a story, he then follows his original story boards—with adaptations—to make certain that the reporting, photography, headlines, and navigation make the stories easy for the reader to enjoy. Little tends toward the storytelling of the *Wall Street Journal* feature articles, which he says works well on the Web. The first page uses an anecdotal lead to draw the reader into the story. The second page broadens the story with the "nut graph," the paragraph that explains the main points of the story. The other pages flow from these first two pages to allow the reader to follow a variety of links that expand on each report. The process is called "layering." Because a computer screen contains much less space than the front page of a newspaper, the first layer or page of a digital story can contain a headline, a digital photograph, and text that makes the user want to continue to the next layer. The pages are usually less than 500 words with the option for the reader with a click of a computer mouse to follow a highlighted path set out on a guide. But *you* may want to follow another path. You could read about the 1860 convention and want to learn more about what was happening in Chicago during that period. After searching through the archives of that time, you can proceed to the next convention or even skip ahead to another convention. The layers provide a logical way to proceed, but the layers can also enable you to read the digital page in any order. "I write the story in chapters," Little says. "What works best is when you have a design on the Web that is the equivalent of the layout of a magazine. Your eye and attention are focused on one part, which is easily digestible, and it flows and leads you into other parts."

Reporter Grumman found her first days at the Internet edition frustrating. She started on the newspaper's print side, where she covered suburban police departments. "My first instinct was to do quick hits," she recalls. "They went nowhere. They were up for a day and, boom, they're gone." Her first attempt at using the Internet for a more complex story involved the murder of a twenty-four-year-old woman in suburban Chicago and the police investigation into the crime. The main story of "Who Killed Stacey Frobel?" appeared in both the on-line and print editions without significant editorial differences. In the Internet edition, however, readers could click on a chronology of events, a list of the people involved in the crime and investigation, and a variety of background stories—far more than would have been available in the daily newspaper. Simply put, no space limitations exist on the Internet because an on-line story can be as long as the reporter and editor think it should be.

When reporter Henderson wears his Detroit Tigers baseball cap, he looks like a young Spike Lee. Henderson studied political science at the University of Michigan and started in journalism as an editorial writer. Within days after his arrival in Chicago, he noticed a story about murder rates in the city. "It wasn't a big deal. It was a story that the paper does every year," he recalls. "I said to myself, 'I bet there's a lot more there.'" Henderson asked the print reporters for all the information about the murders—the times, the neighborhood, the cause of death, and a variety of other statistics. He put together a map of the city and allowed citizens to look for information about their neighborhoods—again, with a click of the mouse rather than a visit to the records office of the police precinct. "We got thousands of people interested," he says. "If we use a big database in telling a story, you also have to give the readers a chance to use that database. That's giving people information that's important to them."

Then he has devised a database for each Chicago public school, allowing parents or students to determine how their school compares with the rest of the city, from spending to reading scores. "The medium really shapes the writing. It makes you write shorter and sharper," Henderson says. "When I worked on the city desk, I would go do my story and I might assign a photographer. Then I'd just pass the thing on. Somebody else edits it. Somebody else copy edits it. Another person would read it and decide whether it would go on page one. Someone would decide where the photos would go. Here it's so much more important for me to be there through the whole process, shaping the thing so that it make sense in the medium."

A portion of the *Tribune* readership attracts a sizable group on the Internet—middle-class men between the ages of twenty-five and thirty-five. As a result, one of most popular sections of the Internet edition is sports, where fans can follow the Chicago Bears and the Chicago Bulls and college and high school sports. Producer Mike Reilley says that "the section becomes your bar stool." The Bulls' page offers an interesting contrast between what can be done on-line that doesn't fit into a newspaper. The pages include a list with stories about every game of the Bulls' season. There's even a reprise of how the fans tore up the city during some victory celebrations. And there's a section on forward Dennis Rodman, whose best-selling book, cross-dressing, and bad-boy antics have attracted readers from throughout the world. "The Bulls and Dennis Rodman have been great for us," says Reilley, a former *Los Angeles Times* reporter.

The next step is taking the stories and sections and putting them on-line. "We looked at the daily paper and said, "What works?' Our brand name—the *Chicago Tribune*—works," explains Andrew DeVigal, the designer of the on-line edition. Next, people have to get around easily, which is called "navigation." Along the left side of every digital page is the "rail," which provides information on every story in the Internet edition. With a click of a mouse, the user can travel to a particular section or story. If you choose a section, the title will turn from red to blue. That shows you where you are.

The major differences between the on-line edition and the printed version are what DeVigal describes as immediacy, interactivity, and multimedia. During the Democratic convention in Chicago, for example, the on-line edition updated stories throughout the day, including the resignation of political aide Dick Morris, who was caught in a sex scandal. In addition, "Buzz" and "Only for Political Junkies" provided offbeat tidbits and gossip of what was happening at the convention, the parties, and on the streets. Interactivity allowed the Internet edition to include a tracking poll of 500 people about President Clinton and GOP hopeful Robert Dole and then asked readers of the on-line edition in an unofficial version how they would respond to the same questions. The results tracked closely with the official poll.

Multimedia allowed users to listen to every speech at the Democratic convention—or the Republican convention if they wanted—through a program known as RealAudio, which stores audio programs for use at any time. Video clips included interviews with ordinary people and delegates from the convention, and a reunion of protesters from the 1968 convention. One technology, BubblePhoto, presented a picture of the convention site with an amazing 360-degree view of the United Center. The viewer could zoom in to take a look at the television network skyboxes or widen the shot to see the entire convention floor.

The bottom line of any publication, however, is the bottom line. The late Robert McCormick built the *Tribune* into his self-proclaimed "World's Greatest Newspaper," the initials from that banner, WGN, became the call letters of the company's radio and television stations. In 1924, the radio station became the first to broadcast the World Series, Indianapolis 500, and the Kentucky Derby. While other newspapers worried about the encroachment of radio and television, the *Tribune* added the new media to its holdings. In fact, the company expanded its radio and television holdings to New York, Denver, New Orleans, Atlanta, Los Angeles, Philadelphia, and Boston. The company has seven of its ten television stations in the top markets and five radio stations. The Tribune Entertainment Company produces programming such as *Geraldo*. In 1991, the *Tribune* began to invest in technology companies, buying a stake in AOL. In 1996, the company also invested $7 million in Excite, a firm that indexes and searches the Internet.

How will the *Tribune*'s new media operations make money?

It's difficult to pry much specific financial information from anyone. So far, the Internet edition has cost several million dollars since its inauguration. Owen Youngman, the director of interactive media for the Tribune Corporation, seems like a high school science teacher behind his glasses, and his nasal-dominated cadence can put some people to sleep. But his zeal for the future makes this son of an evangelical minister come alive. "My neighbor on one side buys the *Tribune* because he's a stockbroker," Youngman says. "My neighbor on the other side doesn't. Why? It's not really fulfilling for someone with two kids in school in suburban Chicago. She cares a lot more about what affects her kids. It's not her fault. It's my fault."

Youngman has a specific business plan that he thinks will make the digital operation a profit center after a few years. "The newspaper business is really good at charging a token amount of money for an expensive product. Fifty cents doesn't cover the paper and ink, let alone the transportation, the gasoline," Youngman says. At many metropolitan newspapers, remember that less than half of a typical budget covers gathering, writing, and editing the news. The rest goes mainly for printing the news, marketing, and delivering the paper to the subscribers. "I could see a day rather than run those big old printers out there," says Youngman, pointing to the press room, "that if you want the *Tribune*, I will buy you a laser printer and put it on your kitchen table and deliver a highly customized version on paper every day if you don't want to go on-line."

The Internet edition is simply one of the *Tribune*'s digital projects. Because the company owns 5 percent of AOL, the *Tribune* has built an on-line site there and has invested $20 million for a $100 million project called *Digital City*, an ambitious project to provide news, information, and entertainment to more than 100 cities throughout the United States from Peoria to Portland. The venture sends a clear signal to Microsoft that big-time daily newspapers are not about to surrender these basic information services to Bill Gates's similar project, *Sidewalk*. Is the battleground between Microsoft's *Sidewalk* and *Digital City*? "I think that's one of the battle grounds," says Youngman. "Because we believe their focus is on entertainment and leisure listings and materials newspapers have always presented." *Digital City* is an ambitious project. The *Tribune* plans to offer more than 300 different sites for towns, villages, and cities near Chicago. Youngman plans to start the on-line sites with what he describes as "horizontal communities," political and geographical locations throughout the Chicago area. Then, he hopes that "vertical communities" begin, with readers interested in subject areas such as religion, parenting, and politics. "Microsoft, CNN, and the *Chicago Tribune* are all going to cover a bombing at the Olympics. Not everybody else is going to worry about Fox River Valley Gardens," a Chicago suburb, Youngman says.

In another ambitious project, the "New Century Network," newspapers throughout the country contribute articles for readers in another part of the country. The network's promotional material says it "aims to marry the interactivity, breadth, and cool conversation of the Net with the credibility and dedicated insight of hometown newspapers across the country . . . and eventually maybe, across the world." So far, a group of media companies that own more than 200 daily newspapers and employ more than 25,000 journalists can provide information from, say, Charlotte, North Carolina, to users in Chicago. Advertisers also can use the group for national campaigns. The initial players include Cox Enterprises, the Gannett Company, the Hearst Corporation, Knight-Ridder, Times-Mirror, the Tribune Company, and the Washington Post Company.

At the *Tribune* and elsewhere, digital journalism remains in its infancy, and there are growing pains. The reporters at the Internet *Tribune* sometimes resemble one-man bands, carrying a variety of technical instruments without the necessary skills to do the job properly. At a printed newspaper, the reporter generally takes a pen, a notebook, and sometimes a tape recorder. At the electronic version, the reporter carriers a pen, a notebook, a tape recorder for audio clips, a digital camera for single snapshots, and sometimes a consumer video camera for video clips. At the Republican convention in San Diego, Grumman sent back videotape after videotape. "You have four things slung over your shoulder," she recalls with a chuckle. "I had to run to Federal Express at 6:45 P.M. every day to ship the tapes. When they got them in Chicago, they said that there was too much movement and too many zooms. It was just a comedy of errors." Digital specialization, where a reporter reports and a photographer photographs, is likely to follow soon. Perhaps more important, there sometimes remains a gulf between those who work at the newspaper and its electronic edition. "When I first was going to the Internet edition, people would nod and say, 'It's the wave of the future,' and they would smile and that was it. They couldn't think of anything to say about it," Grumman sniffs. "People think it's an interesting diversion. A toy. It's not meaty. But it's another way for people to get their news." There also is resentment among some print reporters because of the huge infusion of capital into the digital technology. "There isn't much money for raises," grumps one writer. And there is some fear that the electronic newspaper may someday replace the printed edition. In one rift, the print newspaper published a series about medical emergencies on airplanes, "Code Blue: Survival in the Sky," which ran in June 1996. The stories ran more than 20,000 words, a daunting task for anyone to read. It was decided that the series should be added to the Internet edition with graphics, audio clips, video clips, and even a demonstration about how a defibrillator—a device to help heart attack victims—works. One well-known journalist criticized the approach of the Internet version as being more gimmicks than news, and copies of the complaint circulated all around the *Tribune*.

At the *Tribune* and elsewhere, there are differences in how reporters react to digital journalism and the future. Researchers have found that reporters follow three different tracks concerning their views about the use of computers in the newsroom. The first group, called the "the benevolent revolutionary," is enthusiastic about new technologies. The second group, described as "the nervous traditionalist," is not. A third group, known as "the serene separatist," does not fear technology but sees little impact on the role of the journalist.[2]

The survey results are not exactly what you would expect. For example, the so-called revolutionaries strongly support the notion that journalism "will depend on good writing, good interviewing, and thoughtfulness." Among those described as traditionalists, a fifty-three-year-old editor interviewed for the survey says he finds new technology "hardly intoxicating—more a pain in the ass with the constant rush of forcing on journalists more than they possibly need or can use." One traditionalist describes his concern that new media will emphasize presentation over information. "Writing is almost irrelevant now." Another reporter complains, "As media become more dependent on high-tech inventions, speed, I fear, will outweigh quality." Still, among all of those surveyed—traditionalist or techie—the journalists maintain that quality of information, not the means, remains the most important aspect of news. Those closest to the electronic product realize the medium must win converts. "This medium is in its infancy," Gentry explains. "There are thousands of ways to do things. We just have to figure them out and convince people we're right."

Being right is important to any news operation. When TWA

800 from New York to Paris exploded on July 17, 1996, killing all 230 people on board, terrorism was immediately suspected.[3] The theories ranged from an explosive device in the cargo bay to a missile that left no trace. A mechanical failure of some sort seemed possible. Perhaps something else happened. The investigation became one of the most complex, expensive, and prominent air disaster inquiries in history. Enter Pierre Salinger. Salinger served as press secretary to John F. Kennedy and as a U.S. senator from California. For many years he was chief European correspondent for ABC News. He uncovered secret negotiations for the release of the American hostages in Iran in 1981. He won awards for his coverage of the Pan Am 103 terrorist bombing in 1988. But he may be best remembered for how badly he reported a story about the explosion of TWA 800. In November 1996, Salinger reported the U.S. Navy accidentally fired a missile that brought down TWA 800. Salinger cited French security sources for his story, which made headlines throughout the world. Only a short time after Salinger made his evidence public, a CNN news crew in France showed him a copy of this document:

Subject: Friendly Fire?

TWA flight 800 was shot down by a U.S. Navy guided missile ship which was in area W-105. W-105 is a Warning Area off the Southeast coast of Long Island and is used by the military for missile firing and other military operations.

Guided missile ships travel all over the world defending the U.S. and they were conducting practice firings up over the top of a Navy P-3 radar plane who was on a Southwest heading about over the top of TWA 800. Evidently the missile is supposed to go over the top of the P-3 and the accuracy of the missile is being measured by instrumentation in the P-3.

There was a USAir flight coming from the Southeast descending towards Providence, RI, that had been cleared to 21,000 feet and the TWA 800 aircraft was restricted to 13,000 feet. The air traffic controller requested the USAir flight to turn on his landing lights with the idea that TWA might see his lights and identify him. At that point, he would clear the TWA flight to continue his climb.

The P-3 was a non-beacon target (transponder OFF) flying southwest in the controlled airspace almost over TWA 800 and made NO calls to ATC. After the explosion, he continued his flight to the west and then called ATC and asked if they would like him to turn around and assist with the "accident"!

You will remember that the first announcement about this accident came from the Pentagon. The spokesman mentioned that they were sending the Navy to the crash site. They immediately sent a Navy Captain who was replaced the next day by an Admiral. That Admiral is still on the scene.

The FBI has conducted at least 3,000 eyewitness interviews and the NTSB[4] has not been able to be a part of these interviews and not have any access to the contents of them. Some of those eyewitnesses reported seeing lights. Those were probably the landing lights of the USAir plane.

It has been a cover-up from the word go. The NTSB is there in name ONLY . . . the FBI is always standing beside or behind . . . it would appear that (the) job is to make sure that nothing is said that would giveaway "THE BIG SECRET!" It is time to end this farce and tell the public the real truth as to what happened to TWA 800. My source shall remain my own but the above information is true and I believe it will all become known soon. Now that all of you know the real truth.

The memorandum—without any original source—circulated on the Internet for weeks before Salinger's report. When shown the copy of the document by CNN, Salinger said: "Yes, that's it. That's the document. Where did you get it?" The CNN journalists got it where Salinger's unnamed source in French intelligence probably got it. They got it where thousands of other people got it. They got it on the Internet, where people can say anything they want to report. But Salinger wouldn't quit. In March 1997, a team of journalists, including the former ABC newsman, filed a sixty-nine-page report in *Paris Match*.[5] The report consisted mainly of radar images that Salinger said he believed "completely confirms that a missile fired downed TWA 800." Salinger added that "we have now reached the point where we are totally sure that what we are saying is true." The lead FBI agent simply replied that Salinger's report was untrue and remained untrue.

When allegations surfaced that President Clinton engaged in sexual relations with a White House intern, the Internet faced another crisis of credibility. The first hint of the scandal appeared in an online gossip column. Traditional media outlets—faced with keeping their Web sites updated with news of the scandal— created special sections online. Individuals published a spate of independent Web sites about the allegations while online chat rooms filled with people who debated whether Clinton should be left alone, resign, or face impeachment.

The incident underlined an important change created by cyberspace journalism. Traditional news organizations faced intense competition on the Internet, making it difficult to refrain from rushing forward with unconfirmed information. In one instance, the *Dallas Morning News* had to issue a retraction for erroneous information it offered on its online edition.

Traditional media face a crisis of credibility among the public. So, too, can digital news and information easily fall into disrepute. Salinger, a traditional journalist, ironically gave the Internet a black eye without even knowing it. But online journalists are entirely capable of creating their own credibility problems, as evidenced by the Clinton scandal. Still, the strategy of publications like the *Chicago Tribune*, which has steadily increased its commitment to digital journalism, aims at meeting the needs of readers from sports fan to city school users and virtually everyone in between. Addressing specific needs of smaller groups of readers can encourage those users to return to a publication that may have lost its relevance.

chapter six

All News, All the Time:
The Internet and Television

If you think the 13,000 guys at Microsoft who aren't
millionaires yet are going to show some restraint,
you're in for a surprise.   —Andy Nicholson,
                                              Microsoft

At Studio 8H at NBC headquarters in New York's Rockefeller Center, a man in a blue work shirt polished the ceramic tile. He arrived on time. A man in his sixties, known as the floor manager, donned his headset. It's his job to make certain a program gets on and off the air on time. As always, he was there early. On July 15, 1996, the news conference to announce the $440 million joint venture between NBC and Microsoft, MSNBC, started more than thirty minutes late. The reporters covering the news conference had time for an extra cappuccino and pastry from the elaborate coffee bar. Apparently, there was a glitch in the computer systems on the new station and World Wide Web site, so the NBC brass wanted to make certain everything worked properly before answering reporters' questions.

Just after 11:30 A.M., General Electric president Robert Wright, NBC president Andrew Lack, and anchors Jane Pauley and Brian Williams walked into the studio. As they put on their microphones, the white-haired floor manager signaled three minutes to air. The cleaning man left for another job in the building. In Washington, NBC anchor Tom Brokaw stood in front of the White House, where he would interview President Clinton later that day on MSNBC. Even Microsoft leader Bill Gates was live via satellite from the MSNBC newsroom in Redmond, Washington. "This won't be an instant success," GE head Wright acknowledged. But he described the $440 million deal as a "revolutionary partnership" and "an evolutionary one."

It was somewhat ironic that a reporter from CNBC, which is owned by NBC, asked Lack, the NBC president, about possible conflicts of interest. Conflicts of interest? Microsoft makes computer software that dominates the worldwide market. General Electric is a defense contractor that owns NBC. Microsoft, GE, and NBC own CNBC and MSNBC. Microsoft owns the Microsoft Network, a World Wide Web service and information provider that has contracts with Hollywood producers, as does NBC. Conflicts? "We are getting used to these conflicts of interests," Lack said with a straight face. "There are land mines everywhere. It comes with the territory. . . . I don't think there are any media companies left in the world not encountering this problem."

Within the past decade, potential conflicts of interest are indeed everywhere. More important, fewer news organizations produce news than ever before. Big is not necessarily bad. Big, however, does stress the bottom line, which can cause the news product to suffer. Just a few years ago in the mid-1980s, television news operations weren't expected to make money. Entertainment shows provided that revenue, and news shows brought respectability and public service awards to the network. That changed. Capital Cities bought ABC and then sold it to Disney. Hotel magnate Laurence Tisch bought CBS and then sold it to Westinghouse. General Electric bought NBC. News now has to make money, too. The news business is a business. It is, however, the only business protected by an amendment to the U.S. Constitution, and an unspoken contract once existed that news should aid the public's understanding of current affairs. That doesn't mean that profit and public service are mutually exclusive, but I recall when one news editor turned to me after a bombing in South America and said, "If the terrorists want coverage, they have to move farther north. Do they really think that anyone's going to cover them down there? It's too expensive."

How big are the media today? Gannett owns nearly a hundred

daily newspapers, including *USA Today*. The combined circulation is nearly seven million readers. The company owns sixteen television stations, five radio stations, and a security alarm system with more than 70,000 subscribers. My only experience with Gannett happened as an intern at my hometown paper, the *Idaho Statesman* in Boise, where the corporation turned a family-owned voice in the community to mush. Profitable mush, however. I must admit that I cringe whenever I see someone reading *USA Today*, which has brought the worst of newspapers and television into a single milieu. And more than a million people read it. Fewer than ten corporations own many of the publications, radio stations, and television channels most people use. It won't be much different in the age of 500 channels or high-definition television.

In less than two years, Microsoft has joined these major media players. What's its strategy? Microsoft does not make televisions. It doesn't even produce computers. But one of the highest stakes games in the next decade will be who controls what you use—the electronics industry with television sets or the computer makers.[1] Right now, television sets use analog technology, which means the signals are usually carried by a cable wire from a broadcast facility to your set. Even if you use an antenna, it's still the same basic technology. Computers use digital technology. Starting this year, consumers will eventually replace every one of their televisions with new digital models. That's a market of at least 230 million new sets worth an estimated $150 billion over the next decade. So Microsoft has cut a deal with Intel Corporation and Compaq Computer Corporation, two creators of computer hardware, for a way to offer a mixture of television sets and computers, with Microsoft to provide software and information. In short, Microsoft is becoming a bit like the media version of Procter & Gamble, the huge consumer products company. Procter & Gamble does not make washing machines or sinks. The company offers a variety of detergents, for example, each of which would seem to compete with one another, but which actually augment and expand its market share in detergents.

Microsoft provides the operating software for nine out of ten computers in the United States. Simply put, that means that Microsoft controls most of what we see on the screens throughout the country. Microsoft Office controls about 80 percent of the total market share for word processing and financial programs. Now add to that the ability to receive programs just like a television set. The arrangement with NBC for a television channel and an Internet site was one step. Now the company has expanded the Microsoft Network to give you information and entertainment programs on those same computers. It should come as little surprise that MSN talks about "channels" on its World Wide Web site—a direct assault on the entertainment programming on traditional stations. Microsoft intends to help you manage your finances, stay informed, make purchases on line, manage your free time, and have fun. Take, for example, one of the first *Sidewalk* Web sites in Seattle. You can find out when your favorite musical group comes to town. You can read about restaurants, including reviews and a copy of the menu. You can tell *Sidewalk* what type of movies, music, and food you like, and it will present custom picks and editors' recommendations. Already, the national advertising sponsors include BMW, Bank of America, Barnes & Noble, Citibank, Club Med, Visa, and United Airlines. Microsoft Money offers personal banking and bill-payment services to seventy-five financial institutions. The latest version of Microsoft Investor offers insights and editorials from industry pundits. You can also view historical charts of mutual fund performance, compare the performance of different funds, and trade through Charles Schwab, e'trade, and Fidelity. The sudden lurch toward media occurred because Microsoft realized that software sales could not sustain the astronomical growth of the 1990s. If you could put news on a desktop, you could make money. And that's what inspired Bill Gates to embrace the media. Within the next decade, Microsoft expects that 20 to 25 percent of its revenues will come from its media holdings.

After the news conference to announce the deal between Microsoft and NBC, I went home to watch the new station. It seems that my cable television provider doesn't offer MSNBC. So I tried to find Brokaw interviewing Clinton on the Internet. It was incredibly frustrating. Three times, the MSNBC Web site froze my computer system. I was persistent. I tried to join the Ask Clinton Forum. But I needed a password, and there was nowhere to show me how to get a password. I finally gave up because I was told I could read the transcript the next day. Unfortunately, the transcript wasn't available then.

It did get worse. Not for me, but for MSNBC. Only two days later, TWA Flight 800 crashed into the ocean off Long Island. Brian Williams, the annointed star of MSNBC and an up-and-coming star of NBC, had a miserable night. MSNBC simply was not ready for prime time. Apparently, no one could figure out how to create an electronic map of the crash scene—a relatively simple function for virtually every television station from Fargo, North Dakota, to New York City. Williams finally had to hold up a map to show where Long Island was located and where the aircraft had crashed. It so happened that Robert Hager, the network's aviation specialist, was in Atlanta for the Olympics. MSNBC went live to Atlanta to Hager, who could tell Williams absolutely nothing new about the air crash that happened a few miles away from Williams's New Jersey studio and a long way from Atlanta.

NBC and Microsoft simply want to use MSNBC as a means to make better economic use of personnel and computer programming. NBC's reporters and correspondents will gather and report the news, airing it over broadcast television and the twenty-four-hour cable news network. The reports will be converted to a different medium—the World Wide Web—that can be accessed by personal computer. Williams, the anchor of the MSNBC network, is an attractive fellow from New Jersey with a rather unimpressive resume. Before joining NBC News in March 1993, he worked as a local reporter in Washington, D.C.; Philadelphia; and New York, where he was the anchor of the noon news. NBC president Lack apparently determined that Williams had the ability to think quickly on deadline, and he's handsome. On the Jay Leno Show, Cher once called him "very attractive in a Republican sort of way" even though Williams worked for the Carter White House. He later spent some time reporting at the White House and is said to be the heir apparent for the evening news anchor desk, if, and when, Tom Brokaw decides to leave. Williams is considered a traditionalist in his news judgment, preferring Washington and international stories to feature stories.

Unfortunately, when you watch the MSNBC nightly news program, it is a traditional broadcast. For example, a recent program led with a story and an interview on Wall Street stocks going higher. Then, a story about television and children. Then, President Clinton, the safety of air bags. Then Madonna. What's different from the other networks? It's an hour rather than thirty minutes. Isn't there a way to break away from the traditional format of you speak, someone speaks, I listen, I'm bored?

On the Internet, however, it's a different story for MSNBC. Brock Meeks, the Washington reporter, is not a handsome guy like Brian Williams. He is a good reporter and a man who takes chances. In 1989, he went to report on the Afghanistan for the *San Francisco Chronicle*. He managed to convince some of the rebels to let him travel with them as they attacked Jallalabad, a provincial capital in Afghanistan. The government troops—without the backing of the Soviets, who had pulled out a few weeks earlier—still had military might the rebels could not match. A rocket attack left the band of sixteen rebels dead, torn to pieces by schrapnel. Meeks took some shrapnel in his side but managed to make it back to a field hospital. Despite the close call, he traveled back with the rebels four more times. After being knocked unconscious during one battle, however, he decided that he should look for safer work.

Meeks had reported on technology before becoming a foreign correspondent, so he traded in his bush jacket and epaulets for a modem and a laptop. First, he wrote for *Communications Week* and then *HotWired*. He produced a column, "Cyberwire," that often took Microsoft to task. "I've been very critical of Microsoft, particularly the business practices, which are predatory and heavy-handed. Because they are such a dominant force, they throw their weight around," Meeks charges. "I don't think they've had the most ethical of business practices." So how does a critic of Microsoft became the Washington reporter for MSNBC, the joint venture between Microsoft and NBC? "I became convinced that it is being driven by the news side," Meeks says. "There are so many things that Microsoft is involved in, they don't have the inclination or the opportunity to be heavy-handed in the newsroom. They're just writing checks."

Meeks and MSNBC on the Internet are trying to provide news concisely and quickly to those tired of the same old formats. "We're as fast as anybody in the world," says Merrill Brown, the head of MSNBC in Redmond, Washington. "We are doing more to tell stories in more interesting ways." At a daily news meeting, Brown has not lost his often-terse New York ways. He has worked for the networks and cable television's Court TV. He scans through the competitors' Web sites on an overhead screen as he listens to his editors in Washington, New York, and Redmond discuss the days events. CNN stands as the main competitor, and he likes how it handled a story on the murder of JonBenet Ramsey, a child beauty queen in Colorado.

Brown listens to a smorgasbord of stories. A commuter plane has crashed near Detroit, killing more than twenty people. Weather problems plague the Northeast. The Dow has moved up 66 points. Brown asks, "What's going on in Boulder?" An editor explains that the Boulder police chief has scheduled a news conference on the investigation in three hours. Barry Clift, a producer, questions why the case has attracted so much attention. "Bad things happen all the time in bad neighborhoods," Clift says. "It's one little girl." A bit annoyed, Brown explains that viewers are interested in stories about the wealthy, stories about mysterious deaths, and the possibility that a relative may have killed her. Brown does listen as Clift makes his points. The Colorado story will get prominent play, but it will not be the lead story. The editors urge that the airplane crash is important, but Brown remarks, "What's going to be new? They'll still be dead." A crass assessment. He suggests that a fitness package be the lead item, arguing that MSNBC should give the users something unexpected. Finally, however, he agrees that next day's O.J. Simpson's opening testimony in a civil case should get top billing.

Since May 1996, Brown has racked up frequent flier miles between Redmond, Washington, the home of Microsoft, and the New Jersey studios of MSNBC and the New York offices of NBC. His first goal was to get the programs up and running. That's done. Now it's time to develop MSNBC as a brand people know and trust. "We are trying to create the world's preeminent news brand on cable and the Internet, and we're trying to create an Internet news service that is technologically more savvy and journalistically way beyond anything else going on," he says. That goal faces some not insignificant hurdles. Bill Gates is both a help and a hindrance. Many analysts think that Microsoft will dominate the news business as it has the software business, and the reviews of MSNBC often reflect that view. "Everyone who reviews us says we don't want Bill Gates to own the world, but

MSNBC is pretty good. Every goddamn lead is the same," Brown says. "I have that hurdle to overcome."

Even insiders admit that MSNBC sounds like a disease, not a brand name. "The difficulty of the brand name is nobody knows what this thing is," Brown admits. "We are fighting a battle against the *Wall Street Journal*, the *Los Angeles Times*, the *Washington Post*, and CNN—big global brand names—where our brand name is the least well known. Even in Seattle, I wear an MSNBC hat and people say they know the NBC peacock thing, but what's the MS?"

98

Moreover, there can be a clash of cultures among the various participants. NBC-GE operates in the pinstripe world of television and defense contracts. Microsoft operates in the Eddie Bauer world of computer programmers and software developers. "You're trying to marry two companies that don't have a lot in common. GE is building jet engines on one hand, and Microsoft is developing software on the other. Different thinking, different coasts, different everything," says David Pawlosky, one of the top editors. "Beneath that you have the culture we're trying to create here: one of journalism. So we had to push them off with both arms so we did not get suffocated by either one."

So far, there have no significant clashes among the three cultures, but there have been a few confusing moments. A computer program, for example, often gets tested in the field. The first or second packages—known as the alpha and beta versions—will have a number of glitches. So Microsoft puts the program on the market and then fixes the mistakes. "We had a bit of a problem explaining that you have to get news right the first time around. You couldn't test it and then fix the mistakes," says one editor. Many people want news on demand that meets their needs, and that's what MSNBC on the Web provides. News is being broken down into niche markets of individuals who will control their own access to the types of information they want and when they want it. "I think the collective experience of news is over: the hearth and Walter Cronkite and all that good stuff," Brown argues. "Everyone has his or her own TV, and the family is not gathering around the TV. There is no nuclear family sitting around at 6:30 every night and sharing a news experience."

So what can the MSNBC Web site provide that we can't get anywhere else? Take, for example, the work of Kari Huus, a photographer, radio producer, and former reporter for the *Far East Economic Review*. Huus traveled to Indonesia just after it was revealed that the Clinton campaign had accepted illegal contributions from Indonesian businessmen. Few Americans know anything about Indonesia except those who recall one of Mel Gibson's first movies, *The Year of Living Dangerously*, about an Australian journalist covering the civil war in Indonesia in the late 1960s. Huus's first report focuses on President Suharto's warning that communism—banned thirty years ago during the civil war that Gibson's movie depicts—has gained strength in the country. She calls Suharto the country's puppet master—a reference to the shadowy relationships in the country among the political elite, the military, and business—a theme throughout Indonesian culture and the Gibson movie. For the past thirty years, Suharto has used iron-fisted authoritarianism to enforce his will. There have been benefits. In 1967, Indonesia ranked as one of the poorest countries in the world with an average per capita income of about $50. Inflation exceeded 600 percent. Today, the economic has grown at 6 to 7 percent a year with inflation at only 5 to 10 percent. Poverty has fallen dramatically, to 14 percent from 60 percent in 1967. Some economists predict that by the year 2020, Indonesia will have one of the world's largest economies.

But there is trouble.[2] At the MSNBC site, you learn that riots occurred last year, and a significant challenge faces the dictatorship. Labor strikes proliferate. With her skills in radio, photography, reporting, writing, and extensive background in Asian affairs, Huus provides a diary of the sights and sounds of Jakarta, the capital of Indonesia, which lies at the heart of an archipelago of some 17,000 islands as wide as the United States. More than 80 percent of the people practice Islam, but there are large groups of Christians and Hindus. "The government has held the whole thing together through a combination of repression and education," she writes. "Jakarta has a population of eleven million, despite government campaigns to spread the population to more remote areas. . . . Although most people have been lifted out of poverty, income disparity remains a serious problem. About 3 percent of the population control at least 75 percent of the wealth. For many people in Jakarta, running water and sewage are still lacking."

100

Few places exist in the popular media where an American can find such background on Indonesia. MSNBC also offers an extensive guide to the players, including those from Indonesia, in the campaign-finance scandals in the Clinton administration. Other special sections provide in-depth coverage of civil war in Zaire (now the Congo) or an interactive questionnaire on an individual's risk of specific types of cancer. To complement an NBC television report on dangerous roads, the MSNBC site gives readers the ability to determine where dangerous roads exist near their homes. At the MSNBC Web business site, there's historical information about the markets, and up-to-the-minute charts and graphics on what's going on. Programs help analyze your stock portfolio, your child's college education fund, and your retirement fund.

"You are asked to do the best of television, the best of radio, and the best of print. To do one well is difficult. To do all three is mind-boggling," says Pawlosky, one of the start-up managers for the MSNBC site and now the commerce editor. Significant problems loom in combining the Internet and television. The World Wide Web remains a text-based medium. It provides good photographs, articles, archival material, and graphics. The Web can do radio clips adequately. Only recently have there been some successful tests to provide video via the Web. The problem is that there's an enormous amount of information required to transmit a television picture. Simply put, there are a lot of zeros and ones in computer programming that make it complicated to move television quickly through the Internet system. Consider this carefully because it's a bit technical: You don't notice it, but there are 525 lines in a typical television screen that move from top to bottom. In one second, the lines move thirty times down the screen. Your eye can't see that. That's the beauty of television. In most video programs on the World Wide Web, the programs move down the screen at rates of fewer than thirty times, or "frames." That means the images on the Web have a herky, jerky quality that make them almost unwatchable. In addition, information moves on the Internet in small packets that travel in a variety of directions in order to go from one computer to another. With so much information, the images could arrive out of order— even in a short video clip—creating a sequence that makes little or no sense. In a thirty second video presentation, for example, the first packet to arrive could come from the fourth section, which comes between twenty seconds to twenty-five seconds into the video clip; the second packet may be from a section that runs from five seconds to ten seconds after the beginning. What you may get is a scrambled version of the original transmission.

Streaming media—both audio and video—deliver material in a steady, continuous flow of news and information, which can begin before the entire program reaches a user's computer. The material is compressed at the source and then decoded at the user's computer terminal with a software program. In short, the stream of information begins playing before the entire program has been downloaded onto the computer, which enables a much faster and less frustrating experience. Again, however, the product leaves something to be desired, primarily because it remains grainy and still can be slow. One writer described the process as "sucking peanut butter through a straw."[3] For example, one minute of CD-quality sound requires 10 megabytes of disk space, which means that one minute takes nearly six minutes to download over a typical modem. Broadcast quality video requires 1.2 gigabytes per minute. With a typical modem, it would require more than one hour to download that single minute. Even using a top-of-the-line business connection, known as a T-1 line, it would take nearly fifteen minutes to obtain the material.

At some point soon, these technical problems will be solved. In the meantime, some news agencies, including MSNBC, do already offer limited video on the Web. But what advantages exist in moving television onto a computer, to simply copy what already exists? I think few. At its beginning, radio copied newspapers. That didn't work. When television began, it tried to copy radio. That didn't work. Each medium finds its strengths and weaknesses. No doubt the Internet will copy television when possible, but the Internet will have to find what it does best. In the mantra of the late media guru Marshall McLuhan, television is a "cool medium," where viewers are passive, taking in information. Moreover, the viewer sits a long distance away from the set compared with a computer, which means that the computer-television must emphasize images rather than the written word because text can simply be too difficult to read from the distance most people watch television. The World Wide Web is a "hot medium," where you play an active role in what you send and receive. The Internet seems far closer to newspapers and radio broadcasts than television in this respect. Certainly, reasons exist to use television methods on the Web, but these methods should not dominate this new medium. That's why the MSNBC experience so far seems like two separate companies, one on television and one on the World Wide Web.

I tend to subscribe to what's known as the "furnace" distribution of news and information. That means there will be one day a digital furnace that collects information. Then the furnace distributes the information to a screen that resembles a television if you want to watch a movie, or to a computer if you want to check out specific details of your stock portfolio. In short, televisions and computers will be integrated into a total information system. Will people want dozens of digital television channels, access to millions of Web sites, or both? I think both. So far, however, MSNBC has had enough trouble melding the technologies of television and the Internet successfully.

Only 40 percent of America's households have computers, but 98 percent have at least one television set. So how do you grab the television market? In Microsoft's view you buy WebTV, a California company that provides a device to connect a television to the Internet for about $300. It provides the equivalent of an inexpensive computer that's relatively easy to operate while providing Microsoft a way to dominate the television market.

Back at Studio 8H in New York, I couldn't help but wonder if Brian Williams, Jane Pauley, and Tom Brokaw will dominate the news we use. MSNBC reaches less than three out of ten homes in the nation, but everyone was convinced about the wisdom of what was happening. Jane Pauley introduced a video montage of her program, a rather unimaginative use of NBC's film and videotape archives. The promotional video included an interview with John Lennon, where he was asked about the Beatles' hairstyles. That got her excited. "People thought the interview was lost," Pauley said. If Pauley and MSNBC get excited about an interview about haircuts, I suspect the American viewing public will find something else to watch. Somehow the melding of the World Wide Web and the cable television should prompt something more exciting. The aging floor manager ended the program to launch MSNBC on time. He did his job well, as he had for thirty years. As the news conference ended, the janitor in the blue work shirt returned to clean up the mess left behind by the anchors, news executives, and journalists who attended the MSNBC extravaganza.

chapter seven

Paying for the Digital Age: Advertising, Subscriptions, and Business

Cyberspace. A consensual hallucination experienced
daily by billions of legitimate operators, in every
nation.   —William Gibson

Robin Miller operates a two-car limousine service in Baltimore, Maryland. When Miller decided to advertise, he explored the best way to do it. An ad in the on-line edition of the *City Paper*, which has 100,000 readers, cost $10 a month with little possibility of business. A fifteen-second spot on the local "classifieds" channel cost $65. A small ad in the local telephone directory cost $1,500 a year. Then Miller turned to a computer science student at the University of Baltimore to put up a site on the Internet. The Web page cost only $25 a month and linked the limo site with information about entertainment events. "I can't make the folks get married, or go to the airport, or the concert. All I can do is make sure that, when they do, they call me instead of some other guy. Am I succeeding? Find a big search engine. Punch in 'Baltimore Limousine Lowest Price,' " he says. Miller's business is booming.

Advertising from small companies like Miller's limousine service and big companies like Procter & Gamble pay most of the bills for many publications and is likely to be the primary source of money to finance digital journalism. Moreover, while advertising may be annoying at times, it also serves as a source of news and information, although it clearly does not meet the definition of journalism because an ad has a point to view and tries to persuade us to buy a certain kind of breakfast cereal or vote for a particular political candidate. Think about how advertising reaches us now. We see an ad in a newspaper or on television. The advertiser builds an image or provides information that tries to convince us to head down to the local car dealer to buy a Ford or to buy Excedrin when we shop at the local supermarket or pharmacy. Many times the information is limited to what can be said in thirty seconds over the air or written in a few lines of print; sometimes we get a catalog with detailed descriptions about clothing or hardware in the mail. The advertiser hopes we actually read the printed material rather than toss it in the trash, but if we do read the descriptions, we still have to place an order on the telephone or stop by the hardware store.

107

The Web changes the relationship for the reader, the on-line publication, and the advertiser. The advertising may not look significantly different at first glance, yet the Internet offers the advertiser the ability to provide vast amounts of information about a product—a feature unavailable in traditional media except with a buyer's handbook. For example, automobile companies are placing more advertising on the Internet. In a television campaign for a car, the company can establish a brand identity and an image, not much else in thirty seconds; think about some famous slogans: "Like a Rock" or "We're No. 1 and Counting." Toyota, in its Web campaign, uses what's known as a "bubble camera," which allows you to zoom in on any part of the car. In addition, there is textual information about the automobile from engine sizes to tire sizes and everything in between. "In broadcast or print media you have to deliver a short message," says new media specialist Regina Joseph. "The Web offers the ability to describe your product any way you want and show virtually any type of image. You can go 300 pages deep if you want to. And if you do it well enough, you can get your message out there in more effective ways."

Another Web advantage: advertisers and marketers can analyze an ad campaign much more precisely than in traditional media. While newspapers can provide numbers on how many people read the publication, virtually no way exists to indicate precisely how many people see the ad. Neither radio nor television can give specific numbers on how many people *actually* listen to an ad. On the Internet, however, the results can be counted immediately. In fact, a body of initial research exists about what works and what does not on the World Wide Web. An ad doesn't work as well on Mondays as it does on the weekend.[1] The best days? Saturday and Sunday. Users click on slightly more than 2 percent of all ads displayed on the Web, a higher rate than direct mailings. Animated ads work best. Messages like "click here" increase the response rate significantly. Giveaways don't always work. Bright colors such as blue, green, and yellow work best; red, white, and black are less effective.

As a result, advertisers are finding on-line publications more and more attractive. In the first six months of 1997, companies spent more than $200 million in on-line advertising. That's triple the amount of money from the previous year but still only a small fraction of what advertisers spend.[2] By the year 2000, however, advertising on the Internet is expected to hover near $3 billion. That's nearly ten times the amount of advertising now on the Web. By the year 2000, one prominent research firm estimates, advertising will account for more than 90 percent of Web revenues.[3]

Starwave, a company in Bellevue, Washington, attracts millions of dollars from advertisers turning toward on-line publications. Starwave offers a panoply of electronic magazines on parenting, entertainment, sports, and news. Backed by Microsoft cofounder Paul Allen and Disney, Starwave attracts specific advertisers for each of its sites. For example, *SportsZone*, a joint venture with ESPN, features sports drinks as major sponsors because the site attracts people in the target audience, says Shelley Morrison, Starwave's director of advertising. "We're seeing bigger and bigger budgets for advertising on the Web." So far, technology companies are the largest advertisers, she says, again because the Web reaches that target audience.

But the Web offers even more. The advertiser can provide the information, track what readers find interesting, and then *close the deal*. On-line buying makes it easy for the reader and the advertiser, and even the digital publication gets a cut. "You want the amount of time between when someone thinks about buying a product and buying the product to be really short. And that's the beauty of the Web," says Morrison of Starwave.

109

Who's buying on-line? Merchants have monitored the emergence of a distinct constituency for on-line shopping—the technical male. Nearly half of those interviewed are seeing repeat purchasers, customers are not just surfing. Personal computers, pornography, compact disks, and small gift items represent more than half of on-line purchasers. Web transactions amounted to about a quarter of all purchases related to travel, such as airline tickets, hotels, and car rentals.

Despite more women being on-line, products that might specifically appeal to women face major hurdles. Cosmetics, underwear, and personal care products are low-priced items that cannot be distributed profitably because of the high cost of shipping. Moreover, clothing often doesn't look appealing on a computer screen because of the mediocre quality of pictures on the Web. Only when high-quality video is available on the World Wide Web will a number of companies turn more and more to the Internet for sales. Another study is a bit more upbeat; it isolated a variety of customers:[4]

> *New Enthusiasts:* In the past year, eight of ten people in this group made purchases on the telephone and one in ten via the Internet. Nearly all of this group has access to the Internet either at work or at home. These are among the country's highest earners with

an average income of more than $50,000 year and are amenable to buying items via computers.

Surfers: Young, upscale consumers are important buyers on the Internet. This group tends to be impulse buyers.

Hopefuls: This group earns less than the average household and has large families. But this group will purchase goods and services if it's easy. Right now, the people in this group makes purchases via infomercials and home shopping channels. But the group may be inclined to make computer purchases.

Faithfuls: This group rates above average in age, income, education, and family size. The report found that the people in this group "are already starting to embrace electronic commerce." The survey added that this finding "is one of the most powerful indications that the future of electronic commerce has the potential to be a very bright one."

Independents: Three out of four people in this group have access to a computer at work or at home, but these buyers remain a tough sell. The survey found that this group wants to touch and see products before purchasing them.

Old-liners: This group is generally over the age of fifty-five and has limited access to computers. This group "serve(s) as a constant reminder that not everyone in America is interested in learning about new technologies or finding new ways to do things." Electronic commerce ranks low on the list of priorities for this group.

Many people do not feel comfortable giving their credit card numbers over the World Wide Web. Ironically, many of these same individuals have no problem providing the same information to a sales clerk, a waiter, or a telephone operator. Forrester found that security perils are mostly perceived, not real. Those business owners interviewed say that security concerns on-line are overblown. "I have been amazed by people not wanting to use their credit cards over the Internet. They are terrified of the technology and the openness on which it rests. But with time and media exposure this will change," says one apparel retailer. His company handles thousands of credit card transactions without a single instance of fraud so far. "It is a misnomer that the Web is dangerous. In fact, I have found it to be pristinely honest," one businessman said.

A further advantage of the Web: the ability to search easily and quickly through databases. As a result, classified advertising—long a key revenue stream for newspapers—may abandon printed publications. Simply put, information can be far more easily found on-line about the right job, apartment, or roommate than in print. Just go to the classified ads of an on-line paper and enter a search word like "engineer" or "bus driver." The computer will provide a list of possible jobs by city, state, or even nationwide within seconds. An apartment? Simply type in number of bedrooms, square footage, location, and price range. A roommate? Nonsmoker with interests in judo, Russian language, and South Carolina. You will probably get a match. Consider the prospects for personal ads, complete with digital photographs. "Newspaper print classifieds are at their peak," a recent study reports, "and from here on out we can expect to see growth slowed each year as new competitors—fueled by emerging new technologies—chip away at newspapers' long-held lock on the classifieds business."[5] In five years, newspaper classifieds may see no growth. That would have a dramatic impact because classified advertising accounts for nearly 40 percent of a typical newspaper's revenue. If revenues from classified advertising should fall by 25 percent, the industry's profits would drop from today's 15 percent to 9 percent. If revenues drop 50 percent, the profit margin for newspapers would be 3 percent. That means a number of printed newspapers would face serious cutbacks, and some papers will go out of business.

But the Web also creates a complication in the relationship between on-line publications and advertisers. Historically, advertisers turned to the traditional media to provide the news content to attract the readers who then would hopefully look at the advertising. On the Internet, advertisers can create their own content, short circuiting the traditional relationship with the publication. Take a look at how Regina Joseph designed a Web site for Microsoft's Close Combat, which became a top seller on the Internet at $50. Close Combat allows you to fight the battle of Normandy on D-Day, the June 1944 invasion that eventually lead to the Allies' victory in World War II. You can use strategy as either the German or American commanders, and there's no guarantee the Allies win. You can play against others in another city or country.

Joseph created the site's own information to advertise and sell the product rather than depending on traditional media. The Web site mixes advertising, marketing, information, and entertainment. The site includes all the weapons used in the invasion with actual sounds and includes photographs and history about World War II battles. "Our mandate was to encourage people to download the demo and then buy the game," Joseph says. "Close Combat is for hard-core military buffs. They are stringent and exacting. You can't fudge it with them."

In Maneuvers, a player receives specific information to make a decision. For example, this battlefield communiqué arrives:

Imperative that you take the schoolhouse at the crossroads. It is heavily defended by group of 352nd infantry. Holding back a major push. Situation critical. Deploy one of your platoons immediately. We must take this position in the next twelve hours.

The options include:

1. Send in Platoon 9. The platoon leader is dead, but the unit has suffered limited casualties.
2. Send in Platoon 15. The platoon has suffered significant casualties, but the platoon leader is active.
3. Send in Platoon 17. The squad leader is active, and the platoon has only suffered limited casualties. The platoon is some 300 yards in rear of the other two squads over difficult terrain.

I chose No. 3. A military strategist and psychologist, Steven Silver, analyzed the choice. "This would be the best squad to use, but it is going to have to do some hauling to get into position for the attack." He points out that the squad will face fatigue when the assault begins. He adds that American troops are usually required to carry too much equipment, which means they could become physically exhausted.

The game uses an artificial intelligence engine to track the possible effects of orders, as well as the responses from the enemy. If you want to check out Silver's reputation, there's a picture and Web page that says he's a former Marine who works for the Veteran's Administration, a computer user, and an avid tactical game player. There's a separate list of his publications on post–traumatic stress disorder.

Why does Microsoft, the king of programming, turn to others to advertise and market a product? "We understand the Internet, and we develop for the Web. We are able to match content with marketing," Joseph says. "The ability to understand advertising and marketing—that doesn't change. You just have to be adapt to the idiosyncrasies of each medium."

While advertising pays the bulk of the costs for putting out a traditional publication, subscriptions pay at least part of the bills. Have you ever thought about how much you spend on the media every year? There's the newspaper. Magazines. Cable television. What about books? On-line services? The average household spends nearly $700 a year, just $125 less than what that same household spends on electricity. When home entertainment media are added, including the costs of premium cable, pay-per-view television, entertainment video rentals and purchases, the annual household spending nearly hits $1,000.

Will you have to add to those yearly costs a payment for the news you want? For the most part, users have been reluctant to pay for many services other than pornography. But some time in the future, publications hope to charge you for your subscription. So far, however, the *Wall Street Journal's Interactive Edition* is one of the few major publications to charge subscribers. Editor Neil Budde saw his circulation plummet immediately from nearly 700,000 to 70,000. He couldn't have been happier because he lost a number of subscribers who paid nothing and gained a loyal following of users, many of whom do not buy the printed version. In addition, the electronic version attracts an audience with an average age in the upper thirties, not in their fifties as the printed version does.

There's almost everything that's in the printed version, but there's more in the cyberjournal. For example, the Internet publication contains a personal edition. The on-line editions provides a personalized stock portfolio updated on a minute-by-minute basis. The Internet edition includes extensive briefing books on publicly traded companies, information that used to be immediately available only to stockbrokers and analysts. In addition, discussion groups exist on news and business topics, a potpourri of opinion on a wide range of subjects from some intelligent people. In short, the Internet edition provides a value-added product for only $29 to $49 a year, which is a significant reduction from the yearly cost of the printed edition. While subscriptions add only a few million dollars, every additional income source props up the bottom line of the *Journal*'s electronic edition.

At Individual Inc., an information service aimed primarily at businesses, subscriptions provide nearly 80 percent of revenues. Individual provides customized services on 4,000 topics to 20,000 companies with 400,000 individual users. Individual Inc. helped develop what's known as "push technology." Simply put, Individual provides a daily electronic mail pushed to a computer much like a newspaper lands on your doorstep. That electronic mail, which requires a subscription, reminds users every day that Individual is ready to provide news and information. That's different than expecting the user to remember to go, or be "pulled," to the Web site. It's a bit like depending on someone to take a trip to the newspaper stand or the local pharmacy to buy the publication. That means an inconsistent revenue stream for both the Web site and the newspaper because some days you simply forget to pick up the paper or visit a Web site. "Consumers of information often need to be prompted or reminded to access something as opposed to remember to get something. The newspaper would not be nearly as strong if there were no home delivery," says Michael Kolowich, chief executive officer. "When the electronic mail arrives on your computer, it's time to get your next dose of information."

Forrester Research estimates that domestic revenues from subscriptions will rise from $1 million in 1995 to $206 million by the end of the decade—still not enough to subsidize the industry. Nevertheless, only two years ago, less than 1 percent of on-line users paid for subscriptions. By the year 2000, more than one out of ten people are expected to pay for news and information.

All told, on-line publications must depend on the traditional ways in which their printed cousins derive income, through advertising and subscriptions. In fact, on-line publications may lure some of the traditional advertisers away from print, particularly the classified business. Moreover, the Web does offer specific advantages, such as better information for advertisers and the ability to offer on-line transactions. But it's important to keep in mind that despite dire predictions, newspapers survived the introduction of radio and television; radio survived the onslaught of television; and it's likely that all media will adapt to the competition for advertisers now that new media are involved in the mix.

chapter eight

The Upside of the Internet

Brothas and Sistas. Not tall enough for the NBA? Too "unique" to get signed to a record deal? Don't worry; there's another way to get outta the ghetto: the Internet.
                                        —McLean Greaves,
                                      president, VM Inc.

It's been a long day for McLean Greaves. Rapper Biggie Smalls was gunned down a few days before, and Greaves has been going through audio and videotape nonstop for two days for a tribute to Smalls on the Web.

Ironically, Greaves then had to turn his attention to the Web site design for Bad Boy Records, Smalls's label, which was supposed to go public soon. Greaves and his coworkers would have to work around-the-clock to get the Web site done. Simply put, sweat equity and long nights are putting their company, Virtual Melanin, on the Internet map. His clients include director Spike Lee's company, 40 Acres and A Mule Filmworks, and the Entertainers Basketball Classic, a tournament held each year in Harlem.

The premier site, however, is Cafe Los Negroes, a cyberspace meeting place for news, entertainment, and chat. All of Greaves's sites emphasize "melanin," or dark pigment. "It's everything on the Web with melanin," he explains, with an emphasis on attracting African Americans and Latinos, particularly those from Generation X. Whites are welcome. It's not an exclusive club. The cafe includes an on-line publication with news and entertainment and sections devoted to poetry, new filmmakers, music reviews, and even a fashion boutique.

Born in Barbados, Greaves grew up on Vancouver Island, Canada, where there were three blacks in his high school graduation class. He recalls buying hair products through mail order from

Chicago because none were available in western Canada. The only time he could hear black music was by turning his radio in a certain direction after midnight to find a Seattle jazz station. So he decided to develop Cafe Los Negroes for those who may not be able to easily access black and Latin culture.

The World Wide Web opens up huge possibilities, Greaves argues, for news and entertainment at low cost to the consumer. Together with Arzie Hardin, a former Wall Street currency trader, and Tyrone Thomas, a top-of-the-line programmer, Greaves has put together a team of about twenty people in design and marketing. Many members of the group live in Bedford-Stuyvesant, one of the toughest neighborhoods in New York City, because it keeps overhead low and allows the group to create a computer literacy among young blacks and Latinos. "We're bringing it right to the streets," he says. "We're basically showing people that they have a voice."

It is not a strident voice. It is confident voice with a good bit of humor. Across the top of Cafe Los Negroes, for example, the site pledges that Ebonics, the street language, "is not spoken here." The company's answering service states: "Remember the next revolution will be computerized." Greaves stresses the need for entrepreneurial skills in the ghetto rather than protests. "It's different from the old rules of the sixties—protests and solidarity," Greaves explains. "We don't complain about 'the White Man.' That's anachronistic. It worked well when there were the civil rights issues of the sixties. But not now."

The group produces an on-line newspaper, *Root Stand*, and an on-line radio program, where Greaves uses journalistic skills learned at the Canadian Broadcasting Corporation. He has started to create a team of camera operators to work on a virtual news site. "In the United States, there's a chasm between blacks and whites. If you tap into our world and hear our debates and our issues, you can join in. It doesn't make any difference what race you are. Even if you say you're white, no one on our sites is going to say, 'You can't hang out here.' "

While Greaves applauds President Clinton's desire to wire American classrooms with Internet connections, he sees a critical need for teachers who can use the technology. That's why his company is teaching a group of inner-city students how to produce Web sites and video. He thinks most families can afford some sort of access to the Internet. Now he and his colleagues need to help establish computer literacy—coupled with interesting content—in order to attract people to news, information, and entertainment on the Internet.

For the most part, many minorities and lower-income families feel cut off from traditional publications that often target middle- and upper-income readers. So experiments in education throughout the country, particularly with younger students in schools, may help create a new audience for on-line journalism. Blackstock Junior High School in Port Hueneme, California, tries to teach computer literacy. Most of the students are Hispanic, and many have trouble with the English language. So the school set up a computer lab—a so-called smart classroom, with nearly thirty computers—to help teach the students English as a second language. But that's not all: seven other classrooms with just as many computers help teach science, history, literature, and business education.[1]

One super-sophisticated laboratory, known as "Tech Lab 2000," attempts to make students comfortable with the technology in the modern workplace. The lab is outfitted with computer-assisted design software and a satellite dish, and a special device enables the teacher to control what's going on with each computer. Students can work on the same project or individual projects. Even outside the smart rooms, the other thirty classrooms have at least ten computers and two printers.

Taylorsville Elementary School in Taylorsville, Indiana, serves about 600 suburban students from pre-kindergarten to the sixth grade. The students are predominantly from lower middle-class, white families. The school emphasizes language arts, math, science, history, and geography and allows students to proceed through courses at their own pace. The school has one computer lab with twenty-five Apple computers. Each of the twenty-five classrooms has a cluster of four student computers, one computer for the teacher, and a printer. Students can access the Internet from computers in the library, and there are plans to provide the Internet connections in each classroom.

Northbrook Middle School in Houston, Texas, serves about 800 students, many of whom are the children of migrant farm workers, in the sixth through eighth grades. The school's primary aim is to teach students to think critically. Teachers assist students in learning how to find and analyze information. With more than 400 computers in the school's six technology labs and forty-eight classrooms, students have at least one computer for every two of them. That's a ratio among the best in the country, which averages about one computer for every five students. Each classroom has a videodisk player, a scanner, and multimedia editing equipment. Teachers receive special training to learn how to integrate the computers into the classroom.

In each of the schools, traditional test scores are up. So is attendance. The students get better jobs, and many go on to higher education. In addition, the annual costs for technology are down. In all three cases, these students would be considered among the traditional have-nots, based on income, and less likely to turn to traditional media for news and information. But who exactly are the haves and have-nots in a digital age? Is it based on income? Rural or urban? US or overseas?

In Washington, the Clinton administration seems convinced that a significant gap exists between rich and poor and that the gap will widen. "We don't want the Internet to be a tool for the rich and the upper middle class," argues Ira Magaziner, a senior advisor to the president. "We want all of our people, particularly all our children, to access the Internet because it is such a powerful medium." Magaziner's three children attend schools in the nation's capital, and each has access to computers. He thinks that government should provide equal access to the Internet. "Education has always been a public function in the sense of support. I think making certain the Internet available is critical," Magaziner argues. "A kid grows up in a poor neighborhood and goes to a school that has less of a tax base to support it. We think it's important to give as much opportunity to that student as a student who can afford to go to a wealthy school." The Internet allows a school in a relatively inexpensive way to multiply its resources dramatically, he says. Instead of buying a library of books, "you can in a more cost-effective way tap into things."

Despite Magaziner's beliefs, much of the data do not bear out his views. Technology *is* penetrating the nation's schools. Three out of four public schools have access to some kind of computer network. More than half can reach the Internet.[2] There are more computers for fewer students, more computer power at lower cost. Students in small and large schools have roughly the same level of access to computers. In fact, a recent federal study found that 65 percent of U.S. public schools had access to the Internet in the fall of 1996, nearly twice as many only two years before.[3] Public schools with high numbers of students in poverty were slightly less likely to be connected to the Internet, but by the year 2000 nearly every public school plans to have access. Nine out of ten schools with Internet access had e-mail and access to the World Wide Web.[4]

Another survey found the average African American student attended a school with 4 percent fewer computers per student than that of the average white student, hardly a significant disparity. "With the price decline in computers and more computers being brought into schools, the Internet is becoming much more accessible," says Hardin of Virtual Melanin. "There may be a gap between blacks and whites, but it's narrowing really fast." That means a growing group of ethnic digerati who are potential consumers for Virtual Melanin and other digital publications aimed at these youngsters now and when they grow older.

All races, creeds, and colors are using the Internet, and news and information remains the first choice for people turning to the digital alternative.[5] Those with higher incomes tend to use the Internet more, but people who earn $30,000 and $50,000 use the Internet at roughly the same ratio as they are represented in the general population. In addition, a survey found that a higher percentage of African Americans than whites planned to access the Internet in the next three months.[6]

Adam Clayton Powell III, a long-time media analyst at the Freedom Forum, sees promise for minorities and developing countries using the Internet. In November 1996, Powell toured South Africa and was amazed at what he found. In Alexandra, a black township north of Johannesburg with no paved streets or running water, Powell found a group of people at the local community center. "They have a battered old machine that they use to hit the Net every night to pull in Web sites of African newspapers to find out what is happening around them. Now these are people who do not read newspapers on paper—they have leapfrogged directly to newspapers on line!" he says. "It is exciting, empowering, and an irresistible force."

In the developed world, programming on the World Wide Web focuses on niche groups such as African American and Hispanic youth. "The Internet is coming to resemble television, especially among the young, who are abandoning broadcast television in droves. And just as we do not talk about the television-rich and the television-poor, the inequalities of Internet access are rapidly becoming moot as it has evolved into a genuine mass medium," he argues. Just after the turn of the century, Powell believes that Internet users will be a microcosm of the U.S. population as a whole.

Is there a knowledge gap between urban and rural areas when it comes to computers?[7] Apparently not. Simmons Market Research found that information technology is becoming more and more equally distributed throughout the country.[8] From preschool to high school, today's children often understand computer technology much better than their parents and a large portion of the adult population. "There's a whole group of people who will never get on the Internet," says Elizabeth Osder of the *New York Times*. "Students today will have a powerful computer on the desk that far exceeds what existed before. That doesn't do anything for the guy who just graduated from tractor trailer school for a good blue-collar career." His children may have access to a computer at school, but his children's needs may be the only way to lure him on to the Internet, she observes.

Age, more than income, may actually divide the nation in the digital age.[9] Jupiter Communications, a New York research company, says the number of children who go on-line will jump from more than four million to more than seven million in 1997, increasing exponentially through the year 2002. MIT's Nicholas Negroponte is concerned about the growing chasm between those who use computers and those who run the country. "There will be almost no digitally illiterate child" by the year 2000, he predicts. Negroponte's describes what he calls the "digital homeless" who run countries, companies, schools, and neighborhoods. "Ironically, the people in control will be out of touch. That is what has to change." Many older Americans may become the have-nots, people who have little desire to use computers or feel intimidated by their complexity. In fact, only 5 percent of those between the ages of fifty-five and sixty-four use an on-line service, and less than 3 percent of those over sixty-five have access to the Internet.

Simplicity is the key, argued the late Edwin Diamond, a longtime media critic and writer who joined the Internet generation in his seventies. He said the computer and the Internet must be easy to use for "a three year old and an eighty year old." He mused that the same is true for videocassette recorders, which only about 10 percent of the American public can program properly. "As for me, I'm a journalist. I use whatever medium available for my messages. If I have to learn how to beam stuff directly into the audience's cortex, I'll do it." But Diamond remained rare among the senior citizens and some seasoned journalists of America, who apparently have little desire to go on-line. Adam Thierer of the Heritage Foundation is concerned about the growing power of the youth over adults. "It's like *Lord of the Flies* in cyberspace—an entire generation of youngsters have been left to fend for themselves in an unknown land. Little parental or elder leadership or guidance is present," he says.

Will those in the developing world be haves or have-nots when it comes to the delivery of news and information in a digital world? In Ghana, Nii Quaynor started out to become a doctor. After one year at the medical school, he realized he was not cut out for the medical sciences. His skills lay in mathematics and in physics and related sciences. Quaynor studied engineering at Dartmouth as an undergraduate and obtained his doctorate in computer science at the State University of New York at Stonybrook. For fourteen years, Quaynor worked for one of the most prestigious technology companies, Digital Equipment Corporation, in management and engineering. The chief executive of the Ghana National Petroleum Company convinced Quaynor, the first individual to earn a doctorate in computer science from Ghana, to take the country technologically into the next century.

Bear in mind what Ghana has faced over the past four centuries. An estimated two million slaves came to the New World from the area between 1500 and 1870. Ghana became the first black African state to gain independence in 1957. But the American- and British-educated Kwame Nkrumah spent massive sums of money on industrialization and public works projects, and by 1966 the country, which had one of the strongest economies in Africa, was badly in debt. After that, Ghana faced military rule and civil war. In 1992, however, Ghana returned to democracy under a multiparty system that encouraged a market-driven economy. "There is no governmental control," Quaynor says. In fact, he adds that the government openly supported his goals to bring the Internet to Ghana and to promote its use. From only two subscribers in 1993, there are now more than five hundred, primarily from people in the mining industry, government, diplomacy, and educational institutions and including nearly a hundred private individuals.

Today, Quaynor is known as "Mr. Internet" in West Africa. He considers as one of his most important accomplishments to be financing the project independently from government handouts or foreign aid. "I did not receive money from the World Bank, I did not take a loan from anybody. It was purely private sector initiative from Ghanaian resources," he says. "All Africa should learn from our model and how we transformed our society." For the year 2000, Quaynor strives for a lofty goal. He wants his company to develop Internet systems for four to six countries in West Africa. The technology, he maintains "will improve business communication internally and internationally." Quaynor wants all of Africa, particularly Ghana and West Africa, to move quickly into new media. "The haves will succeed, and the have-nots will fall behind. Hence, the struggle we have waged to get our country connected quickly in order not to fall too far behind," he says. "The service must be made available at affordable prices in remote regions."

One barrier in Ghana, as in other developing countries, is that access to the Internet goes through the telephone system. Today, only three telephones reach every thousand people and only 37 out of the 110 national districts have telephone access. "We don't have enough telephone lines, so we are installing an Internet satellite to boost our services," Quaynor says. The Internet also depends on computers, which many individuals cannot afford. Some analysts see the Internet, particularly e-mail, as a potential boon for African universities, allowing the schools to access news and information from top libraries throughout the world. "For a university student in Africa, access to those foreign libraries could be crucial," writes professor William Wresch.[10] In fact, Microsoft founder Bill Gates sees Africa as an important market for his company.[11] "The Internet is the single most important tool that will open Africa up to the rest of the world. It is the future of communication worldwide, and Africa is not as far behind as some people believe," Gates says. Microsoft is expanding in Africa, using South Africa as a base; it has opened offices in Kenya and the Ivory Coast and plans to open ten more in the next three years. Africa does lag behind the developed world in its use of computers and the Internet. In the United States, there are 300 personal computers for every 1,000 people, while in South Africa—by far Africa's most on-line country—the figure is just 34 per 1,000. "Technology is not a choice . . . the individual level will take a long, long time, but because we are patient and take a long-term view, we were willing to come in now and build up that infrastructure," Gates says. Here again, the developing world offers a huge market for those who want to provide news, information, and entertainment through a digital medium—a market that only exists today for a few international publications, some television programs, and American movie studios.

In Cambodia, Sophana Meach preaches the mantra of expanding news and information from the Internet. He was ten years old in 1975 when the Khmer Rouge started a reign of terror in Cambodia in which more than two million people died. Sophana's father worked as a land surveyor in the local government and was executed within days after the takeover. So Sophana traveled to the northern jungle with a family friend, who told authorities that the child was an orphan she had raised. The Khmer Rouge had determined that children needed no education; "having rice, having everything" was the government's mantra back then. Sophana was assigned to a work crew, which started the day at dawn without breakfast. The daily food ration included a bowl of thin rice soup and sometimes a vegetable soup. The Khmer philosophy was that if people had to worry about finding food every day or the possibility of execution for any transgression, it was unlikely that they would think about much else.

Sophana had to keep secret his father's work as a land surveyor for the government. He told officials that his father repaired bicycles and his mother sold fruit. "Many children in my brigade were executed after the news was sent from the villages that their fathers or mothers confessed or were found out as ex-officials or soldiers of the previous governments," Sophana recalls. "I thought that one day it would be my turn."

Meanwhile, the brigade worked harder and harder. As hunger grew more intense, some children stole chickens and fruit from the nearby collective farms. If caught, they were sent to concentration camps or killed on the spot. One day, Sophana and his work crew were digging a canal. Nearby was a vegetable patch with ripe pumpkins. Meach stole one and cooked it later and shared it with others. "It was so delicious that I have never had such a taste again." The next day he tried to steal another pumpkin, but a soldier caught him. The man tied Sophana's hands and feet and started to interrogate him. Frightened that he was going to die, Meach started crying. The soldier struck him and sent for the brigade leader. That night the children gathered around Sophana at the camp and were ordered to beat him. "I felt somewhat relieved that they didn't kill me immediately. They started to torture me and laughed at me. I didn't know who punched me. Some children merely touched me. I thought they were my friends who pretended to punish me."

Sophana says he survived by telling stories to the younger Khmer Rouge followers in the camp, mainly the plots of Kung Fu stories and adventure books he'd read. By providing information and entertainment, Sophana escaped the torture and death that many of his fellow Cambodians faced. After the Khmer Rouge fell from power, Sophana eventually became an assistant to the mayor of Phnom Penh and a leading figure at Cambodian television. In 1994, he became Cambodia's first Fulbright scholar in two decades and arrived at New York University, where I taught, to study journalism. At first, he rejected my suggestions that he study on-line reporting and design. I argued that Cambodia and other developing countries could benefit from the new technology. Reluctantly, he agreed. By 1997, he had returned to Cambodia an evangelist to the Cambodians, teaching them how to use computers to obtain news and information. "I use e-mail to contact people all over the world. I can contact people to learn about specific issues or technical issues," he says. "I can almost obtain all sorts of information I need. I can read the *New York Times* on the Net. I can read CNN news if I missed any specific program." Sophana has become a storyteller once again, passing on his knowledge and skills for finding stories to his countrymen.

Since Sophana's conversion, I have worked with a variety of

international groups and scholars in an attempt to spread the word of the Internet. Dan Zhang, a reporter from Beijing, spent a semester at New York University and mastered the fundamental techniques of Web design. He works on one of his country's first Web sites. Wei Joo Ng, a reporter from Singapore, came to NYU to find ways to improve on-line journalism in his country. He wanted to convince his editors to invest money to enlarge the newspaper's existing site, but his bosses were concerned that expanding the service would allow users to access pornography on the rest of the Internet, a violation of the law in Singapore. Wei devised a solution to the newspaper's problem by using a filtering system to block out pornography—a requirement that troubled him—while providing a better on-line publication. French and Czech researchers visited me, concerned about the American dominance on the World Wide Web. The editor of the *Shanghai Youth Daily* could hardly contain his delight when I showed him how his readers could find an on-line site for "Hootie & the Blowfish." An Australian scholar asked me to read his presentation, and it took only thirty seconds to get his fifty-page paper via the Internet. A Cuban scholar read my syllabus on international reporting, which includes a study of the 1962 Cuban missile crisis, and he sent me his notes on what he saw as a foot soldier during the crisis; another scholar put me in contact with two generals involved in the nuclear showdown.

The Internet and the World Wide Web have created new communities of people, communities that know few geographic boundaries. Individuals can reach one another almost instantaneously. Information is available for educational courses. Undergraduate and graduate courses are offered in business, humanities, and sciences to thousands of students. The network allows students to use home computers to write papers, do research, and communicate with faculty and fellow students through electronic mail and on-line lecture conferences via the Internet.

Clearly the Internet offers vast opportunity for individuals and digital journalists to share news, information, and entertainment, whether they live in the suburbs, the ghetto, or the developing world. But what about the potential perils? Is there a downside to the Internet? What about a dark side of the Internet?

chapter nine

The Downside of the Internet

A computer lets you make more mistakes faster than
any invention in human history — with the possible
exceptions of handguns and tequila.   —Mitch Ratcliffe

134   There are indeed some significant roadblocks on the digital highway. In fact, the Internet faces what some are calling its own version of the four horsemen of the Apocalypse:

War: Hackers and cyberterrorists who launch attacks against government computers and individuals to disrupt the flow of information.

Death: Traffic overload and system crashes that either slow or impede access to information.

Pestilence: A computer problem known as the "millennium bug" that could cause the loss of a significant amount of data and information beginning January 1, 2000.

Famine: A dearth of specific addresses on the Internet that may impede the ability of businesses, news organizations, and other groups to communicate with one another.[1]

War

September 19, 1996. "Hackers Vandalize C.I.A.'s Web Page"[2]

The Central Intelligence Agency's World Wide Web site was attacked by hackers who vandalized the home page sometime between 6 P.M. Wednesday and 5:45 A.M. Thursday, when an anonymous caller informed CNN of the break-in. The CIA's home page was replaced with graffiti.

*

November 7, 1996. "Troubles on Election Night"

At least one or more hackers tried to close down the *New York Times on the Web* during election night. While the attack slowed service, the *Times* was able to fight off the attack.

February 13, 1997. "Hackers Go on TV to Show Perils in Microsoft's Active X"[3]

135

In a staged appearance on German national television, members of the Chaos Computer Club of Hamburg demonstrated how a Microsoft program could effectively pilfer funds from one bank account and deposit them in another.

February 19, 1997.[4] *"Computer Hackers Clog Capitol Hill"*

Unknown hackers sent hundreds of electronic-mail messages to federal lawmakers over just a few days, in an apparent attempt to clog up Capitol Hill computer systems. The e-mails, which arrived with forged return addresses, warned: "All files on the Senate's computers will be deleted by our gang of cyberpunks dedicated to the eradication of your systems."

FBI Director Louis J. Freeh admits that "computers are the new way that criminals and terrorists have found to achieve their objectives." The goals: to either disrupt the free flow of critical information or to use that information for illegal ends. Either way it means that consumers will face impediments to getting what they want and probably will pay more because businesses face mounting costs to make computer systems secure. At an international computer conference in New York, the FBI director cited three recent cases in which a computer was the weapon used to commit crimes against a bank, the flying public, and a 911 system. In one case, a hacker in St. Petersburg, Russia, nearly gained access to millions of dollars in a U.S. bank. In another case, a convicted terrorist used a laptop to plan attacks on a dozen U.S. airliners. A Swedish hacker shut down a 911 system in Florida for an hour, crippling the networks responsible for responses by police, fire, and ambulances. To combat computer crime, Freeh says that the FBI trains its recruits in firearms and computer firewalls. "We chase fugitives over fences as well as (in) cyberspace now."

136

The Internet makes an appealing target for terrorists, thieves, and malicious pranksters. Using digital weapons takes advantage of the openness of the Internet. Nearly every computer can be accessed from another computer. Hackers can destroy data and alter computer systems. The hackers' weapons come in a vast arsenal. The oldest and best-known software weapons, computer "viruses," come in all shapes and sizes, from prank messages to electronic forms of the Ebola virus. According to McAfee Associates, a maker of virus detection and protection software, as many as 10,000 viruses may be in circulation. An estimated 300 to 400 new viruses are created and circulated each month. That's a dozen or so new ones every day, and electronic mail may be the easiest way for you to get a virus.

Some viruses infect your computer's "boot," or start-up system, so that you can't use the computer. Others infect the files that launch or run your software, rendering the programs unusable. Still others erase your computer's setup tables, which tell the computer exactly what type of machine it is. Whatever the case, these viruses mean you have lost the ability to communicate, at least temporarily.

"Worms" reproduce themselves to fill up memory and hard disks. Worms are often designed to send themselves throughout a network, making their destruction active and deliberate. "Logic bombs" are codes that detonate on specific dates or with a set of instructions, damaging the information on a single computer or on an entire network. Often left by disgruntled employees to wreak havoc later, logic bombs are difficult to find. "Bots," short for "robots," are designed to rove the Internet and perform specific tasks; a newsbot, for example, might fetch news you want from a search engine such as Yahoo. Bots also can be deadly. Cancelbots can erase newsgroup messages; on September 22, 1996, for example, Usenet groups lost about 25,000 messages to racist cancelbots. "SYN attacks," including one known as a "denial of service," involve sending a torrent of connection requests—the same sort you make every time you sign on to a Web site—to targeted sites. Simply put, a SYN attack creates a major traffic jam at the site, often cutting it off to users. That's what hackers tried to do to the *New York Times* on election night. SYN floods are spreading because they require only simple programming.

How vulnerable are those who face an attack? A security expert found recently that many Web sites can be easily penetrated, including those operated by the government, financial institutions, and the media.[5] Computer specialist Don Farmer launched probes on 660 bank sites around the globe, including more than 300 North American on-line newspaper sites, nearly 300 credit union sites, nearly 50 U.S. government sites, and nearly 500 Internet sex clubs. He found that 6 out of 10 sites could not effectively combat a hacker attack. "I barely electronically breathed on these (computer) hosts," Farmer says. With more sophisticated methods, he estimated he could crack 8 out of 10 sites. Farmer separated security flaws into two categories: a red category where a site was "essentially wide open to any potential attacker" and a yellow category deemed less serious. The news media were the most vulnerable. The sex clubs were the most secure. Of the 660 bank sites, nearly 7 out of 10 were deemed vulnerable. More than 6 out of 10 of the federal sites had significant security troubles. More than half of the credit unions proved vulnerable, but only 1 in 5 faced serious security problems.

How serious is the potential of an attack? All told, hackers cost businesses worldwide an estimated $800 million in 1995 through break-ins to computer systems at banks, hospitals, and other large businesses.[6] Despite the staggering losses, few businesses report the security breaches for fear that negative publicity could scare off customers. More than $400 million of the losses occurred at U.S. businesses. A mere threat can be as effective as an actual attack. Within the past year, several U.S. banks have reportedly paid six-figure fees to buy off hackers who cracked the banks' security codes. Defending against such attacks has prompted many corporate users to boost budgets for security. A study conducted by The Yankee Group, a Boston-based consulting firm, and Infosecurity News showed that corporate security budgets have already increased by 25 percent with even more money expected to be spent. Many corporations and institutions are cutting themselves off from the Internet, sealing their information transfers to keep outsiders out. The Defense Department and U.S. intelligence officials have warned companies about replying to requests from foreign governments. A report from the National Counterintelligence Center warns that "all requests for information received via the Internet should be viewed with suspicion."[7] The Defense Department also wants increased security on the Internet, particularly the development of software that will automatically trace hackers. In addition, the department also has called for laws to allow it to attack the computers of attackers. In fact, the Advanced Research Projects Agency, the original home of the Internet, is developing what's called an "electronic immune system" that could detect invaders and launch counterattacks against them, disabling those who launch viruses into computer systems.

Death

Robert Metcalfe isn't exactly a household name. But he's one of the pioneers of networking computers. Because of what he's done and who he is, Metcalfe is taken seriously by many in the computer industry. So when he wrote in his *Infoworld* column that the Internet would face a blackout of service before the middle of 1997, people listened. So far, the system has suffered brownouts, cutting off users and shutting down news sites like the *New York Times* and the *Chicago Tribune* when AOL collapsed for nineteen hours in 1996, but not a full-scale blackout. The "World Wide Wait" may once have seemed like a clever saying. Today, it seems like waiting on the Web outstrips time actually spent exploring the Internet for news and views. Much of the congestion has occurred because of the speed at which the network is growing. It's called the "bandwidth problem." Remember that the Internet originated as a system to link scientists' computers. This network backbone served its original purpose, handling a trillion or so bytes a month in 1991 before the World Wide Web caught the public fancy. By 1994, traffic increased nearly twenty times. Today, it's believed that fifty times more information is flowing through the Internet backbones and growing rapidly. Simply put, too many people are trying to put too much information through the Internet system, which was designed to send and receive textual materials, not today's multimedia extravaganzas.

For individual Internet users, the most noticeable problem occurs when traffic tries to move through one of the Internet's narrow arteries all at once. When you look at a page on the World Wide Web, information is usually sent in at least a dozen packets through five separate networks. The address of the Web page is sent from a computer through a modem or designated line to an

Internet service provider. The provider sends the information to the national backbone providers, usually AT&T, MCI, Sprint, or BBN, which then may send the information to another backbone provider. Next, the second backbone provider goes to the Web site's Internet provider and from the provider to the Web site. Then the information has to return to your computer, following another route similar to the way the original request was directed.

The problem isn't really on the main highway. It's on the on-ramps and small roads leading to and from the highway and then into your office or home. Here are some numbers that tell the story. The superhighway backbone lines move 15,000 pages of text or thirty minutes of video on one line every minute. That means 300 books in a minute, or a full-length movie in about four. Cable modems, which allow a computer to use a cable television line, can transmit or receive 3,300 pages, or ten books a minute. It does take twenty minutes for a movie. That's still not so bad. Few people have these new technologies, and it's not coming to your house anytime soon. Many businesses, including news outlets, have dedicated lines that can transmit 500 pages, or a fairly good-sized book every minute. But moving pictures are a problem. For every minute of video, it takes a minute on the computer. That's still fast by home standards. If you want to pay a lot of money for a digital telephone line at home, you can receive forty pages of text every minute. So now you're down to a chapter. You can only get five seconds of video every minute. But few people want to spend hundreds of dollars for a digital line at home. So most people use a telephone modem. These transmit or receive about five to ten pages of text a minute. To receive about one second of video takes one minute.[8] "I proudly tell my family, 'Isn't that great!' " says Richard Duncan of Time Warner, "and they scratch their heads and say, 'But it's so slow.' "

Technology companies plan a whole bunch of gadgets to try to solve the bandwidth crisis, and telephone companies are adding more capacity. For the immediate future, however, more and more people will be frustrated by how long it takes to download that favorite site on the Web. Metcalfe and others are concerned that some solutions must be found quickly. Otherwise, the communications system that supports the Internet and World Wide Web may collapse locally or even nationally when too many people collide with too little bandwidth. "Bandwidth to homes is the bandwidth problem. Competition is required to drive it," Metcalfe insists. He points to outages at Netcom On-Line, AOL, and BBN, where millions of people lost service, as examples of the vulnerability of the Internet. But he also acknowledged the catastrophe he'd projected has not yet happened. During a speech to an Internet group in April 1997, Metcalfe heard the crowd chanting, "Eat, baby, eat," reminding the computer guru of his pledge to eat his magazine column if the collapse didn't take place by spring 1997. Metcalfe tore up the column, put it into an electric blender, and downed the liquid goo. Still, he's convinced that bad times may lie ahead. He thinks his prediction was simply premature.

Pestilence

In the movie *The Day the Earth Stood Still*, Michael Rennie, who played an emissary of the worlds from outer space, tried to warn the Earth that it must stop its movement toward nuclear war. As an indication of his power, Rennie created havoc by literally making nearly every automobile, train, and engine stand still. At midnight on January 1, 2000, known as 01/01/00 in most programming languages, many computer networks may stand still. Perhaps it will not be as dramatic as Michael Rennie's signal, but it will certainly create havoc.

Back in the 1960s, the elimination of every digit saved valuable space on a computer's memory. That space could be used for other information. Programmers created the now-familiar mm/dd/yy format for dates, which eliminated the "19" in 1998 and made it simply "98." Unfortunately, once every 100 years, software cannot account for the change in centuries. In short, "00" will mean 1900, not 2000.

Just how serious is the 2000 bug? Take a look at this possible scenario. It's Saturday, January 1, 2000. You turn on your computer and get an invalid date reading. You switch to another PC that boots up and dials in to your Internet service provider. But you're denied entry because of unpaid bills dating back decades. With another provider, you get on the Internet, but the news sites you've visited daily are gone. Whole networks have disappeared. Your electronic mail system is confused, too, with the newest messages all the way at the bottom. You try to buy something on-line, only to be told that your credit card has expired. You check with your electronic bank, and you discover your password has expired. You have a serious case of the millennium bug.[9]

Despite plenty of warning, the millennium bug may find users woefully unprepared for its onslaught. Some computers will be crippled; others will behave oddly. Whatever the case, it will cost a lot of money to solve this problem. The most conservative estimates start at $200 billion. In addition, the original code for many applications was lost long ago, making the applications uncorrectable. Some older languages such as variations of COBOL, Pascal, and FORTRAN have fallen into disuse, which means that finding programmers to fix the systems will be difficult and costly. Unless these systems are reprogrammed and repaired, critical information will be lost.

At the Internal Revenue Service, the government doesn't know precisely how bad the problem will be.[10] The best estimate now is the IRS has to plow through millions of computer codes and 30,000 applications spread across 300 to 500 minicomputers and 100,000 microcomputers. So far, the IRS has the worst part of the peril defined: 62 million lines of computer code in 19,000 computer programs that comprise the guts of its main data center in West Virginia and other key systems in its field offices. The military operates nearly 10,000 computer systems running more than 100,000 programs. It will cost more than $1 billion to fix the millennium bug. That estimate does not include all the costs of fixing computers at the National Security Agency, the CIA, and the Pentagon's supersecret weapons programs. Bruce McConnell, a senior official of the Office of Management and Budget working on the year 2000 problem, expressed confidence that the government's most important systems will be working properly before January 1, 2000. "I don't think we'll get everything done, but I hope we'll get everything done that has to be done," McConnell says. But one analyst said most organizations probably underestimate the magnitude of the task. "It's like one of those Whack-a-Mole games at the carnival," says Bruce Hall, research director for Gartner Group. "Problems keep popping up faster and faster."[11]

The government is not alone in fighting the 2000 bug. At Allstate Corporation, in Northbrook, Illinois, programmer Dan Deco stares at "K7" on his computer screen.[12] "Right there," Deco says as he points at the spot. "That's what the year 2000 problem is all about." K7 is a minuscule piece of computer code unique to Allstate deep within the company's mainframe-computer system. Deco and more than a hundred programmers must pull out and repair all of the pieces of programs dealing with dates, while making sure everything else doesn't crash down around them. Allstate hopes the job will be done by end of 1998, when it begins mailing renewal notices for one-year policies expiring in 2000.

On this morning, Deco is electronically thumbing through a

mainframe scheduling program named ARCANo2 when he finds K7. He determines the field involves a date, but before he can fix K7 Deco needs to know which of Allstate's half-dozen different date formats was used to create K7. No one knows how many thousands of other bits of code like K7 remain hidden inside mainframes at Allstate. One of the main troubles is a computer programming element known as "fields." Fields are routinely used in programs as a temporary stand-in for a piece of information, and they can represent anything: a name, address, balance due, or date. The fields act about the same way that variables like x do in algebra. Today, there are specific rules about the names programmers can give fields. A field that represents today's date, for example, might get the name "TDATE." But in the past, a programmer might have called the same field "NOW." In earlier computing days, programmers created fields named after rock lyrics, flowers, and sweethearts. These fields pose such a problem because there are so many of them, for example, Allstate's mainframe computers use 40,000 separate programs, totaling about forty million lines of code. Each program can contain dozens of different date fields. Because the names of these fields are so different, there is no way to know which fields are associated with dates except by searching through the entire mainframe library almost field by field. "It's like some huge, weird puzzle. You split it into pieces, and everyone gets their piece," Deco says. In the end, protecting the nation's second-largest insurance company against the glitches will cost at least $40 million. "The problem must be addressed now," admits Joe Thompson of the General Services Administration, which runs computers for the federal government. "If we don't fix the problem, systems will fail. Data will be corrupted. Business will not be as usual."

Famine

Remember when there were only 800 numbers? Now there are 888 numbers. What happened? The telephone companies simply ran out of 800 numbers. The Internet faces a similar problem. Every computer system needs an identification number to communicate on the Internet, and there may not be enough to go around. The engineers of the original Internet designed it to allow different types of networks to communicate with each other through sets of instructions called "protocols." The heart of these protocols are the Transmission Control Protocol (TCP) and the Internet Protocol (IP). Together they are called TCP/IP, and they allow more than a thousand different protocols to communicate into a relatively seamless way that let you go anywhere you want on the Internet.

145

The Internet and the World Wide Web are a bit like an electronic U.S. Postal Service. Every site on the Internet has its own IP address. Everything on the Internet depends on these numbers and on their accurate and rapid recognition by the routers that actually route, or direct, traffic. Rapid expansion of the Internet in the past four years has created massive overload on the routers, and a new standard for numbers will have to be created. Experts predict a collapse as a result of router overload could be just five years away if the Internet's growth continues at its present pace and will happen even sooner if the rate of growth increases. That means you might not be able to even reach your favorite news site, or it will take forever to download it.

One approach might be to eliminate unique addresses for every computer system, requiring them only for networks of computers. In the meantime, engineers are working on ways to manage the system more efficiently, easing some of the burden, and buying time for a wholesale revision of how the Internet handles addresses. It won't be easy. Changing the way the Internet works means not only upgrading or updating every router but also ensuring that every computer on the Internet—that's every computer—is updated.

As you survey the Internet landscape, many positive elements come to mind: easy access to information from throughout the world, discussion groups about a variety of subjects, and the ability to search myriad sources on virtually anything. Yet there are a growing number of factors that may restrict our ability to search far and wide. Hackers, bandwidth, the millennium bug, and identification numbers may cause increasing frustration at the imperfections of the Internet. More important, some may turn away from digital information entirely, leaving the new medium with users who either left or never tried to log on. Will the dark side of the Internet cause it to lose even more people?

chapter ten

The Dark Side of the Internet: Pornography and Privacy

Civilization is the progress toward a society of privacy.
The savage's whole existence is public, ruled the laws
of his tribe. Civilization is the process of setting man
free from men.   —Ayn Rand

Victor and Sharon Lopatka lived in a ranch-style home in Hampstead, Maryland, a suburb of Baltimore. In 1996, Sharon decided to start a business from her home. The thirty-five-year-old Lopatka spent hours on the Internet, trying to drum up clients. At first, she sold psychic advice. She tried to sell advertising for 1-900 telephone services. Then, she turned to offering sex on the Internet. Lopatka tried to sell videotapes of women in the "most exciting bondage fantasy for you . . . to watch and enjoy privately in the comfort of your own home." For several months she posted messages on the Internet to groups concerned with sexual fetishes, bondage, torture, and sexually dominant women.

Sharon spent hours in chat rooms on America Online, where people can send messages to one another. These messages are usually anonymous, so people can describe themselves in any way they want. At times, Sharon claimed she was 5-foot-6 and 121 pounds even though she was four inches taller and 60 pounds heavier. Sometimes, she said she was a 300-pound dominatrix who promised discipline in sexual relations. At other times, she became Nancy Carlson, a woman prepared to star in whatever type of sexual video someone desired. In September 1996, she entered a chat room and apparently became infatuated with a person who said he had a fetish for torture. He used the nickname, "Slowhand," on the computer network. He claimed he was a good lover and prepared to fulfill anyone's wishes. Sharon and

Slowhand wrote nearly 900 pages of notes to one another over the next month. The notes included some of Sharon reputed desires to be mutilated, tortured, and killed.[1]

On October 13, 1996, Sharon Lopatka drove her Honda Civic to Baltimore's Pennsylvania Station. She told her husband she planned to visit friends in Georgia. Instead, she took a train to Charlotte, North Carolina. There, she met her on-line companion in person, Robert Glass, a computer analyst for the Catawba County government. Glass and Sharon Lopatka drove about eighty miles through the back roads of North Carolina to his aqua-and-white trailer home near Collettsville, where he had lived alone after his wife left him six months earlier and taken their three children with her. Back in Maryland, Sharon's husband was concerned a few days later when he found a note from his wife. "If my body is never retrieved, don't worry," she wrote. "Know that I am at peace." He found e-mail messages from Slowhand and gave them to police. After learning from AOL that Slowhand was indeed Glass, police camped outside his home nearly two weeks after Sharon left Baltimore. One officer noticed newly turned dirt about 75 feet from the front door of the trailer. There, police found Lopatka's body. She had scrapes on her breasts and neckline; her wrists and ankles were bound; and there was a rope around her neck. Police charged Glass with torturing and killing Lopatka. He maintained that she died accidentally during rough sex.

149

Was the Internet to blame? Hardly. Sharon Lopatka could have advertised in newspapers or met a man at a local bar. Would the newspaper or the bar owner be blamed? Unlikely. But this incident and other recent events underline the fact that a dark side exists on the Internet. It involves pornography, hate, and invasion of privacy. Once you go on-line, it is almost impossible to steer clear of the dark side. As television executive Roger Ailes puts it, "There are a lot of loonies pressing computer keys out there."

Are there more loonies on the Internet than in society as a whole? Probably not. But some awfully strange people prowl on the Internet. In Minnesota, for example, a convicted pedophile used a prison computer to secretly compile a list of children for other molesters. The files included the names of 99 children in a rural town of 900 people in Fertile, Minnesota.[2] The children's files appeared by name, age, and location and included personal details such as "latchkey kids," "speech difficulties," "cute," and "Little Ms. pageant winner." Those on the list ranged from one-month-old babies to children in their early teens, but most were girls between three and twelve. The towns where the children lived were alphabetized and coded by locations on a map.

It is difficult to determine how, and if, the Internet can or should be regulated. Simply put, there are few laws that govern the Internet. The law prevents child pornography from being made, sold, and distributed in any medium, including the Internet. Some states regulate pornography on the Internet. In Virginia, for example, the law forbids state employees from using computers at work to visit sexually explicit sites. In New York, posting indecent material in cyberspace to anyone under eighteen years old has become a crime. Both laws face legal challenges that the statutes violate the U.S. Constitution.

Existing law centers on what is designated as "obscene" rather than "pornographic" with respect to newspapers, magazines, and film. In order to be considered obscene under the law, the content must depict sexual acts, masturbation, bestiality, or other active promiscuity rather than material that simply sexually excites the reader or viewer. If authorities determine that the material has literary, political, or scientific value, the content may be considered legal. The definition of literary, political, or scientific merit, however, can vary from state to state, city to city, and town to town. Unlike pornographic magazines, the Internet provides immediate and international access. If the owner of a pornographic bookstore sells a magazine to anyone under eighteen, the seller would be violating the law almost anywhere in the United States. So far, that's not the case on the Internet. In one section of a major computer magazine, there are the usual pitches for printers, laptops, and a variety of paraphernalia. There's another pitch, too, for pornography on the Internet.

> "Your computer has never done this before! You control the Action, as a hot live nude stripper obeys your every command! Live on your PC!"
>
> "Choose from a menu of Fantasy girls and pick the ones you wish to interact with."
>
> "Gay Men!"
>
> "Love View."
>
> "The Lace Network."

Each ad gives an address on the World Wide Web. When a user gets to the Web page, there are usually two choices: click if you are eighteen years old, or click if you are under eighteen years old. In addition, the Web contains easily accessible sites on mutilation, even one that shows video clips of people being killed. More than 400 Internet news groups discuss issues from bondage to illicit drug use to advocating violence. In an apparent effort to protect children from pornography, Congress, with the support of the Clinton administration, passed the Communications Decency Act (CDA). The law imposed fines of up to $250,000 and jail terms of up to two years for those who use "interactive computer services" to post indecent material to areas where it could be viewed by those under eighteen. The American Civil Liberties Union and a number of news organizations immediately challenged the law. Joe Shea, the editor of the on-line newspaper the *American Reporter*, printed a direct challenge to the law.[3] A retired Texas judge and assistant professor of criminal justice at the University of Texas at San Antonio, Steve Russell, wrote a screed in the *American Reporter* clearly intended to violate the law. The article read in part:

SAN ANTONIO, TEXAS—You motherfuckers in Congress have dropped over the edge of the earth this time. I understand that very few of the swarm of high dollar lobbyists around the Telecommunications Bill had any interest in content regulation—they were just trying to get their clients an opportunity to dip their buckets in the money stream that cyberspace may become—but the public interest sometimes needs a little attention. Keeping your eyes on what big money wants, you have sold out the First Amendment. First, some basics. If your children walked by a public park and heard some angry sumbitches referring to Congress as "the sorriest bunch of cocksuckers ever to sell out the First Amendment" or suggesting that "the only reason to run for Congress these days is to suck the lobbyists' dicks and fuck the people who sent you there," no law would be violated (assuming no violation of noise ordinances or incitement to breach the peace). If your children did not wish to hear that language, they could only walk away. Thanks to your heads-up-your-ass dereliction of duty, if they read the same words in cyberspace, they could call the FBI!

In May 1996, *Harper's* reprinted much of the article. While the *American Reporter* could face prosecution under the CDA, *Harper's* receives protection under the First Amendment based on previous court rulings. "I don't like to use that language," says Shea, who notes that the only other time foul language appeared in his publication occurred when a book review quoted a salty characterization by labor leader Walter Reuther. Russell's commentary, Shea says, aimed at determining if the CDA could pass constitutional muster. "There is no justification for prohibiting the same speech one uses in a newspaper or in a magazine from publication on the Internet," he says.

Society faces a delicate balance between the community's right to achieve acceptable standards, such as zoning laws and speed limits, and curbs on an individual's right to free speech. General agreement can be reached easily to restrict some behavior: murder, rape, robbery, burglary, and arson. But can freedom of speech, which the courts often also interpret as the same right provided to the press, be restricted on the Internet? Much of what will be done to, about, and by the Internet revolves around forty-five words, the First Amendment to the U.S. Constitution: "Congress shall make no law respecting an establishment of religion, or prohibiting the free exercise thereof; or abridging the freedom of speech, or of the press; or the right of the people peaceably to assemble, and to petition the Government for a redress of grievances."

More than 200 years ago, the framers of the Constitution had no idea that the Internet would exist. Neither could they forsee radio or television. So how does the First Amendment apply to the Internet? What exactly is the Internet under the law? A newspaper, a magazine, a broadcasting network, or something entirely different? Legal interpretations under the First Amendment protect newspaper and magazines to a far greater extent than other traditional media. For example, the government cannot prevent a newspaper or magazine from publishing an article, an action known as "prior restraint." In 1971, the Nixon administration tried to stop the *New York Times* and the *Washington Post* from publishing a secret analysis of American involvement in Vietnam, a study that became known as "The Pentagon Papers." The administration argued that publishing the study would damage national security. But the U.S. Supreme Court ruled unanimously that the government could not prevent the newspapers from publishing the report.

For radio and network television, however, government restrictions are far greater. In 1934, the federal government decided to issue licenses to radio and television outlets because of limited amount of space, or bandwidth, on the electromagnetic spectrum. The licenses, which can be withdrawn if a broadcast outlet violates FCC guidelines, aimed at preventing one signal from disrupting another signal. No such licenses exist for print publications. While there seems little justification for such restrictions today because adequate bandwidth exists, the licensing continues. In addition, the FCC can prevent broadcast outlets from using so-called indecent materials, or objectionable words and pictures, during time periods when children may be listening or watching. Fines have been imposed, for example, against shock jock Howard Stern.

154   Cable television stations receive licenses for specific geographical areas but face few restrictions because subscribers need to specifically request services that might be objectionable. Telephone companies are considered common carriers, so they are not held responsible, for example, if someone uses the service for criminal activities.

When the U.S. Supreme Court heard arguments about the CDA on April 2, 1997, the justices clearly realized the significance of the case, particularly in trying to determine whether to apply existing law or create a new set of guidelines for the Internet.[4] "Isn't it possible that this statute is unconstitutional today," asked Justice Antonin Scalia, "but won't be unconstitutional two weeks from now?" Justice Stephen Breyer repeatedly expressed his concern the CDA would consider teenagers who use the Internet to talk about their sexual experiences as federal felons. Justice Sandra Day O'Connor expressed her concern about phrasing in the law that prevented an individual from "knowingly transmitting indecent material." She suggested that use of word "knowingly" would be exceeding difficult to define. Justice David Souter asked whether parents could be imprisoned for letting their kids look at pornographic material on-line.[5]

When the justices ruled the CDA unconstitutional in June 1997, most news accounts might lead a casual reader to consider the law's opponents on the winning side at the legal equivalent of Waterloo, Dunkirk, and D-Day combined. The *New York Times* proclaimed the decision as "sweeping." One columnist argued that the justices had determined that the Internet was the electronic equivalent of Speaker's Corner in Britain's Hyde Park, where anyone can say virtually anything without fear of legal reprisal. But some experts seemed a bit less sanguine about the meaning of the court's decision. "This is the court dealing in a rather limited way with one particularly badly written statute," argued Michael Froomkin, associate professor of law at the University of Miami. "This is closer to you-did-it-wrong than you-could-never-do-this." Keep in mind that the CDA was a hastily written law that underwent no legislative hearings. Not surprisingly, the Court chastised Congress for vague legal definitions of "indecent" and "patently offensive" material on the Internet. Such definitions are critical to any statute. In short, the Supreme Court determined what will be allowed on the Internet *so far*. Moreover, the Court did not specifically define *what* the Internet is. Without such a definition, the ability of digital journalists and editors to navigate the Internet remained somewhat uncertain except for the ability to distribute pornography or use profanity. So far, it appears that the justices do not believe that the Internet is as invasive or pervasive as radio or television. Therefore, it is unlikely that a minor would be exposed to indecent materials as easily on the Internet as on radio and television. The analogy for the Internet? The Court found it's similar to "dial a porn," where people pay money to talk about sex on the telephone. In a case decided last year, the justices determined that dial-a-porn telephone services should not be restricted because of potential, but improbable, access to minors. While Neal J. Friedman, a computer law specialist for Pepper and Corazzini in Washington, D.C., viewed the decision as a clear victory for the media, he worried about language that could encourage regulation of the Internet by an agency like the Federal Communications Commission. "That gave me a chill because it seemed to be an invitation to Congress to put the regulatory authority in some agency," he says.

Furthermore, the main centrist of the court, Justice O'Connor, and a leading conservative, Chief Justice William Rehnquist, dissented from the majority in the 7–2 ruling. In her opinion, Justice O'Connor opened the possibility for "adult-only" zones on the Internet. Could three other justices in what has been generally considered a conservative court join the two dissenters if the definition of indecent materials was less vague than the CDA and there was the technical ability to restrict access to minors? Democratic Senator Patty Murray of Washington believes so. "The Supreme Court leaves open a large vacuum," Murray argues. "The answer must be workable for industry, it must withstand constitutional questions, and most important, it must provide parents with the option to monitor the material their children see on the Internet."

Even those who in principle oppose censorship of the Internet face some important individual quandaries. Take Brock Meeks of MSNBC, for example, one of the plaintiffs in the CDA case with a long list of credentials opposing censorship. "I've lately found that my staunch anti-censorship principles are becoming battle-scarred, especially when they collide head-on with my own kids and their initial ventures into cyberspace," he writes.[6] Meeks found that one of his adolescent sons downloaded pictures of partially clothed women from America Online. In addition, AOL had shut off the account because of actions that violated the company's "terms of service" rules because someone had used profanity in a chat room discussion. His two boys claimed that their friends had actually been at the keyboard when the profanity occurred. "I felt I had little other recourse than to play censor, a role that caused no small amount of cognitive dissonance for me. Had I turned into one of the foaming-at-the-mouth, anti-pornography types that so revile me in my day-to-day reporting on these issues?" Meeks says. First, he cut off access to chat rooms, allowing access only to "teen appropriate" sites. Second, Meeks prevented the boys from downloading any pictures. Finally, he sat down and had a talk with his sons about the dangers of some people lurking on the Internet. He did relax some restrictions when his twelve-year-old son protested that Meeks no longer trusted them. "I'll continue to battle those here in Washington in favor of Big Brother Censorship," he maintains, "and at night, I'll lie awake, and battle my own parental censorship demons."

157

Some experts contend that filtering software may make cyberparenting a bit easier. Nevertheless, simple tests show these filters far from foolproof. *Consumer Reports* examined the top brands in its May 1997 edition. The magazine chose twenty-two adult sites and put the filters to the test. Cyber Patrol missed six of twenty-two sites. Cybersitter allowed access to eight locations. Net Nanny blocked none of the adult sites. SurfWatch performed the best but still missed four pornographic selections.[7] In another test, one computer program had difficulty discerning the pornographic content of the "Deviant Dictionary."[8] Finally, the filtering program announced a "violation," shut down the system, and recorded the misdeed. One program blocked material on Anne Sexton, the poet, because of the three-letter combination "s-e-x" in her name but failed to prevent access to explicit nudity. The same program also blocked a search for information on Sri Lanka, described as an "exotic" country, that the filtering system seemed to consider either erotic or offering exotic dancers. Microsoft's Internet Explorer, a Web browser, comes with a security system offering parents the ability to restrict viewing of sex, nudity, foul language, and violence. The system can be programmed, for example, to allow "provocative frontal nudity" or hold the line at "frontal nudity." The program will permit "clothed sexual touching" or stop at "passionate kissing." The parent can block all violence from "killing with blood and gore" but allow fighting. The filters have to be updated constantly. *Consumer Reports* found that Explorer allowed access to nineteen of twenty-two adult sites.

Many technology professionals predict that the Internet will face some sort of regulation, primarily because that's what a majority of the public wants. A recent nationwide poll found that almost 50 percent of those questioned favored government restriction of speech on the Internet. Nearly one in three said they believe the First Amendment "goes too far" in protecting freedom of speech.[9]

State and local authorities have already restricted on-line communications. The University of Oklahoma suspended access to sexually explicit discussion groups, called "newsgroups," to ensure that students under the age of eighteen could not access news or information from the sites.[10] The university established two separate sets of access to the Internet: one that censored sexually explicit sites (Server A) and a second that did not (Server B). Federal Court Judge Wayne E. Alley ruled that the university did not violate the First Amendment. "The result of this policy is to allow recreational use of Internet services on the 'A' server, but to restrict the use of certain newsgroups to academic and research purposes," Alley wrote in a seven-page decision. "The limitation of OU [the University of Oklahoma] Internet services to research and academic purposes on the 'B' server is not a violation of the First Amendment." University president David Boren, a former Democratic United States senator, supported the censorship. "The university did its best to strike a very careful balance in order to protect legitimate academic and intellectual freedom while at the same time assuring that the university does not act as a distributor of obscene materials, which (are) not protected by the First Amendment," he said.

Today, many public libraries—a key source of news and information for many in the digital world—are grappling with the issue of whether to restrict access to the Internet.[11] In the capital of Texas and home to the state's main public university, Austin, public libraries have installed filtering software to block access to potentially objectionable sites. Library director Brenda Branch says she believes she has no choice but to install the programs after receiving reports of patrons using library computers to view sexual material. In one case, a library patron used the computer to view images of young children engaged in sex. "No professional librarian ever wants to compromise intellectual freedom in any way," Branch says. "I am trying, in addition to supporting the First Amendment, to deal with the legal, ethical, and moral issues arising because of some of the kinds of things that are available on the Internet and out of my control." The American Library Association opposes the use of filtering software in public libraries because technology often fails to discriminate between newsworthy sites and pornographic material. For example, American Online banned the use of the word "breast" at one point. That blocked steamy chat room conversations about breasts, but it also meant that breast cancer could not discussed. AOL changed its policy.

In Boston, Mayor Thomas M. Menino ordered that filtering software be installed on all city-controlled computers where children have access. That included public libraries and schools. Menino acted after a local city councilwoman complained that children in her district could view pornography in a local public library. On the other hand, patrons of the Los Angeles public library system, which has sixty-six branches and the main library, find quite a different attitude. A notice on the library's own Web site informs users, "The library has no control over the information on the Internet and cannot be held responsible for its content."

Freedom of speech under the First Amendment is often synonymous with freedom of the press. In fact, court decisions limiting freedom of speech almost always affect the way the media can operate. Can speech be restricted? Of course. The classic example: someone yelling "fire" in a crowded theater when no threat exists. An individual is not protected from the law in such a case. But should freedom of speech be restricted on the Internet? Take, for example, this posting to the newsgroup alt.conspiracy in September 1996. The posting, which was titled "Time to Die for God? Or Armageddon—which side are you on" proclaimed that the time for judgment had arrived. Many groups, the post continued, believed that the end of the world was near:

160

> Some examples of those whose ideologies suggest that they have CON-NECTED MENTALLY, cover a broad spectrum—from the Weavers at Ruby Ridge, the Branch Davidians at Waco, the Unabomber, the Order of the Solar Temple, Aum Shinri Kyo of Japan, the Freemen of Montana, to UFO believers, and others. Many like these are still in hiding, while others take the form of the patriot/militia movements, Farrakhan and the Nation of Islam, the many other Islamic movements, and countless groups that are simply rebelling from the system, the "norm," and WANT TO GO TO GOD, OR LEAVE THIS CORRUPT WORLD, at any price.

A member of the Heaven's Gate cult signed the post. A few months later, thirty-nine cult members committed suicide. The Heaven's Gate cult used a Web site and discussion groups in an effort to sell videotapes to try to convince people to join them to reach "a higher level." Fortunately, the message moved only two individuals outside of San Diego to follow Heaven's Gate leader Marshall Applewhite's call for mass suicide.

There are other examples: hate does not dominant the Internet and the World Wide Web, but it certainly is prevalent.The Web page of the Aryan Female Homestead states: "Are you white and proud? Are you sick of the multi-culturalism that is being forced upon our children on the 'jew-tube' in Amerika today? How about the race mixing that has become so popular in the monkey infested cities?" The Knights of the Ku Klux Klan offer an on-line application for membership. At the "Nigger Joke Center," the word "nigger" is defined as "an African jungle anthropoid ape of the primate family pongidae (superfamily cercopithecoidea). Imported to the United States as slave labor in the late 1700's–1800's, these wild creatures now roam freely—while destroying the economic and social infrastructures of America." There are antigay sites, skinhead discussion groups, antiwhite groups, anti-Jewish groups and myriad others with few restrictions. In 1997, AOL decided that it *would* allow the home page of the Ku Klux Klan Realm of Texas to continue operating. AOL determined the site and the ideas expressed were not "hateful or inciteful" and, therefore, did not violate AOL's terms of service contract. The Realm of Texas site states: "America has been cleverly deceived by the lies of the race-mixers and mongrelizers into believing an insane notion—that two peoples can occupy the same place at the same time in harmony." The Web site contains links to the national Klan headquarters that states: "America should be owned by Americans—not Japanese, Arabs or Jews." Another link goes to the Ku Klux Klan's Realm of Ohio page, which refers to "faggots" and "kikes."

161

Should these sites be protected under the First Amendment? Will they be protected? The questions go straight to the issue of the media providing a forum for unpopular or minority viewpoints. Some argue that the media must not ignore the views of all of the public, and in some cases, the airing of offensive opinions may actually diffuse the potential trouble those ideas may cause. In short, the publication provides a kind of release valve to allow the steam to escape rather than having the pressure build up inside the social equivalent of the home radiator. "No one is forcing any of us to be in this marketplace of ideas. But once we inject ourselves into it, we must be prepared to encounter ideas we find objectionable—just as someone might find our ideas objectionable," argues Eric Meyer, a consultant on on-line issues. The sites "are in very poor taste or downright objectionable. But they are not illegal. Nor should they be. The fact that you or I don't like them is irrelevant. That is precisely the type of expression that needs protection."

162

In some instances, however, I believe that freedom of speech should be restricted on the Internet. I don't buy the slippery slope argument that restricting the speech of one individual could potentially affect us all. What if an individual advocates criminal activity, hate, and racism? The Heaven's Gate posting advocated suicide, which remains against the law throughout the country. The organization also urged individuals to follow the actions of groups that had violated the law, in some cases seeking the violent overthrow of individual governments. Again, there may have been a violation of the law. The group should have been investigated and possibly prosecuted under these statutes, irrespective of freedom of speech. The posting represented the equivalent of shouting fire in a crowded movie threater when no threat existed.

Secondly, racism and hate have no place in any public forum. In the workplace, these comments violate federal regulations. In society, actions such as those suggested in the sites could be prosecuted. No media outlet, including a news organization or the Web, should allow these groups to promulgate these beliefs. All Internet providers should ban individuals and groups from providing information that emphasizes racism and hate. If the providers don't do it, the government should restrict such speech.

Here's another free speech case in South Dakota: In December 1996, the governor wanted a small, Michigan-based Internet service provider, Technology Dimensions, to block the account of one of its users. The governor faced an e-mail protest from a digital artist and Native American named Ishgooda, who organized a protest against what she maintained—apparently erroneously—

was the governor's plan to prohibit groups larger than forty people from holding ceremonies on state land. Ishgooda, whose name means "dabble with fire," is a member of the American Indian Movement's Cyber-Support chapter. E-mail attacking the governor's position quickly started streaming in from around the world. Ishgooda forwarded the e-mail to the lieutenant governor, the Parks and Recreation office, the Wildlife Division, and the South Dakota state office of information services. Each organization received more than 300 pieces of mail. State government officials, annoyed at the volume of mail, asked the service provider to shut down Ishgooda's account. The company's service manager asked if the messages were vulgar or threatened to harm anyone. When the state officials replied that no vulgarity or threats were included in the messages, the manager said the missives were "perfectly legal." The company did contact Ishgooda about the matter but stopped short of turning off her account. Subsequently, the governor's Web site used filters to block the company and Ishgooda from sending messages to the state government. In effect, the government of South Dakota refused to accept criticism from a constituent. The governor's office defended the action by calling the e-mail protests nothing but "junk mail" and equated the blockade with telling the post office to stop delivering offensive letters.

Here the issues seem clear as well, but the outcome should be different. If the government of South Dakota can restrict the distribution of commentary by an individual, can the state also restrict the flow of information from a newspaper? Perhaps the government does not like the reporting of the *Sioux Falls Argus Leader*. Should the state government have the legal right to ban the newspaper from all state offices? Of course, the state should not. Banning Ishgooda from sending electronic mail could conceivably enable the state to restrict other complaints from the public and the press, violating the intent of the First Amendment's protection of an individuals right "to petition the government for a redress of grievances."

Another critical issue facing the Internet, the public, and the press is individual privacy. One example can be found in a Texas Internet provider that refused to turn over information about members of a secessionist movement who used the service.[12] The movement, known as the Republic of Texas, maintains that the 1845 annexation of Texas is illegal and that only a popular vote can legalize its status as part of the nation. Charging everyone from Governor George Bush, Jr., to private citizens with the illegal seizure of property, the organization flooded state courts with lawsuits. Just before a small group of Republic of Texas members faced down police in May 1997, Texas Attorney General Dan Morales served subpoenas on ten Internet providers who do business with the the separatist group. The attorney general intended to stop the group from posing as a government entity and clogging the courts with the lawsuits. The subpoenas demanded copies of all members' e-mail, log-in and user identifications, subscriber applications, and billing information, including credit card and checking account numbers. The Overland Network, a small ISP with 100 customers, refused to provide the information and sued the attorney general to stop the order. Compliance with this subpoena would have violated federal law, specifically the Electronic Communications Privacy Act, argued the ISP's owner, Todd Jagger. "This is not a Republic of Texas issue," Jagger told his customers. "It is an Internet and customer rights issue. Our position and actions would have been exactly the same for any of our customers." In fact, Jagger said he didn't support the Republic of Texas group and didn't agree with the political stance of its members.[13] Jagger added that he would comply with authorities if their requests did not violate federal law. Shortly thereafter, law enforcement officials wanted to isolate the Republic of Texas rebels during the armed standoff in May 1997. That included cutting off the electricity, fax, telephone, and Internet access. Jagger agreed to cut access because extraordinary circumstances limited the group's right to free speech. But he insisted that turning over records to authorities violated the rights to privacy of those who belong to the group and those who simply communicated in some fashion with the Republic of Texas. "On the one hand, I'm cooperating and helping out local law enforcement, and on the other hand, I'm having to sue the attorney general to protect basic customer privacy," he says.

The Internet provider took precisely the correct actions to question the right of the government to seek records without specific examples of criminal activity. In fact, the group had sought to resolve its grievances in court. When the group used illegal tactics, the Internet provider took the proper action again by cutting off service. Here again, the government actions pose a potential source of friction with the press and its ability to report the news. The government could seek the electronic records of a media organization in a civil or criminal case, which is allowed in some states and prevented in others when it comes to printed documents and reporters' notes. In the case of a news organization that also functions as an Internet provider, the incident underlines the new and difficult legal landscape a media outlet may face.

Another example involving the individual privacy issue is the case of Chris Kantzes.[14] With his consent, the *Minneapolis Star Tribune* profiled Kantzes, who had recently moved to Minneapolis, based simply on information from the Internet. The newspaper found that Kantzes had posted about seventy-five messages in the past year on Internet discussion groups. From those messages, a profile emerged. He worked as an electrical engineer at Fisher-Rosemount Systems of Burnsville. He earned a bachelor's degree from the University of Delaware and a master's from Syracuse University. A native of Salisbury, Maryland, Kantzes attended plays at Theatre de la Jeune Lune in Minneapolis. He enjoyed radio personality Garrison Keillor and had a passion for microbrewed beer and good restaurants. He wouldn't trade in his Macintosh for Bill Gates's fortune. He called Indiana, where he spent some time in college, a "socially repressive state." He had recently vacationed in Paris and Rome.

"Usually, I try to be careful when I do post," said Kantzes, who was picked at random among Twin Cities Internet users for the story. "I probably should not have been quite so negative about Indiana, although I am very happy that I moved out of there." His home address and telephone number were available. Although the *Star Tribune* published the article with Kantzes' permission, the report provides an example of just how much personal data can be collected on the Internet. In some states, the public and the press can access a variety of data, including driver license records. Electronic telephone books can locate your name, telephone, and home and e-mail addresses within seconds anywhere in the United States and Canada.

Potential invasions of privacy concern Microsoft's Bill Gates— a private person with a significant public presence.[15] Gates recalls that when he was young libraries used removable cards listing the name of everybody who checked them out. He admitted that he liked to see who had read a particular book. "But the cards also represented a modest invasion of privacy. Your past choices of library material, including books on personal topics such as politics, health, even sex, were recorded publicly."

Public records, which often appear in the media, include voter registration lists, tax assessment rolls, water and sewer bills, Department of Motor Vehicle records, securities and limited partnership filings, Uniform Commercial Code filings, federal tax liens, complaints to police, arrest and conviction records, lists of people with unpaid parking tickets, court proceedings and judgments, bankruptcy and probate records, and lists of births, deaths, marriages, and even pet licenses. Many records are supposed to be confidential, but can be compromised. These include credit reports, income tax records, Social Security records, job and housing applications, loan applications, bank account records, credit card records, telephone company records, military records, educational records, and medical records. "With the rise of computer databases and now the Internet, it's getting easier to correlate information to develop a profile of somebody," Gates says. "Despite whatever controversies arise, it won't be long before a lot of information is available on-line." Retail stores need to check an individual's credit. A life insurance company needs access to medical records before issuing a policy. A bus company should check traffic and criminal records before letting someone drive children to school. "Access should be denied to people who don't have a legitimate reason for the information they seek," Gates argues. "A nosy neighbor shouldn't be able to check your credit rating. A curious relative has no business with your medical records. Society must define the appropriate purposes for specific kinds of information and fashion ways to confine the use of the information to those purposes."

Many Internet sites require registration. Not only do the organizations then have your name, address, and some personal information, but subscription services could literally track every article you read or screen you view. One day, someone could use all that information to piece together a detailed personal profile. "You will pay a lot for privacy," says Neil Budde, editor of the *Wall Street Journal Interactive Edition*. "The more you want from the Internet, the more you give up privacy." Budde recalls an e-mail from an individual who did not want to provide stock symbols for a service called "Personal Journal," which allows a reader to choose specific topics of interest. You also can choose to set up a stock portfolio, and the service will monitor price fluctuations and provide news stories. The user who contacted Budde was concerned that the *Journal* could access his portfolio and know what trades he made. In fact, the *Journal* could do that, but it had no plans to do so.

Should you expect what appears on your computer to be private? Should you have the ability to prevent information from coming to your computer? Unfortunately not. Every morning I receive electronic mail from a variety of sources—colleagues, news organizations, and friends. One day, I turned on my Macintosh and found an unsolicited electronic mail. The seller had gotten my e-mail address from a discussion group about journalism. This is what I received:

Subject: Hi
Date: Fri, 27 Sep 1996 23:13:49-0400
From: Friends06@aol.com

Now available for both IBM and MACINTOSH.
MONEY BACK GUARANTEE

The Virtual Girlfriend and Virtual Boyfriend are artificial intelligence programs for your IBM PC or compatible and also for MACINTOSH.

You can watch them, talk to them, ask them questions, tell them secrets, and relate with them. Watch them as you ask them to take off different clothes and guide them through many different activities. Watch and participate in the hottest sexual activities available on computer, including: several sexual positions, using many unique toys, even bringing in multiple partners. This is no doubt one of the most realistic, sexually stimulating computer games available. They will remember your name, birthday, your likes and your dislikes. Every time you start the program, they say different things, and act differently.

Each time, they have a different personality. With the VGA digital graphics, The Virtual Girlfriend and Virtual Boyfriend software have some of the hottest, sexiest graphics out there. And with a Soundblaster or compatible card, you can actually hear their voice as they talk to you. This is the first adult software title that was designed for both heterosexual and homosexual people.

A few days later, I got another unwanted message:

Subject: Paradise
Date: Sat, 7 Dec 1996 08:14:21-0500
From: ChrisMSW1@aol.com

This is to inform you about the new adult game that VCS Magazine rated "The best game of '96" and gave an "Outstanding ****" (4 stars). "The Search for Paradise is no doubt one of the greatest XXX Adult games available." The first game where it is as much fun as it is a turn on. Travel the world to every continent, every country you can think of, and meet some of the most beautiful women in existence. These women will treat you like a king and obey your every command. Any sexual wish you can think of, these women know it all. There is a different paradise for every guy out there, and this game will have them all. This game uses real models, digital video, and digital sound to make it as realistic as possible. You will feel like you're in the same room as the girl you're talking to.

The last adult game we are going to inform you about is the newly released "Club Celebrity X". Imagine being in a club with some very beautiful, well known, ACTUAL celebrities that with skill, will be making you breakfast in bed the next day. These girls you have seen on television, magazines, and billboard ads, and now they are on your computer, begging for action. Each girl you will recognize and you won't believe your eyes when you got them in your own bedroom. This game is hot, and once you start playing, you won't be able to stop.

Software arrives is a plain, unmarked, brown package. Delivery takes no longer than 7 to 8 working days. Both your e-mail address, and mailing address are NOT added to any mailing lists whatsoever. Once you are mailed this e-mail, your name is deleted from all lists to ensure you are not mailed again.

These advertisements are what's known as "spam" in Internet jargon—unsolicited e mails. An individual or company can accumulate e-mail addresses from discussion groups and then send out spams to the addresses from anywhere on the Internet. By posting any message to a discussion group, your e-mail address gets displayed. Information exists as a two-way street, and once you're on the highway you'll find people who don't always play by accepted rules.

How can you protect your privacy on the Internet? Not easily. Some filtering devices can restrict the flow of unwanted mail, but again the instruments have flaws. Ultimately, there is only one choice to protect yourself and your children: turn off your computer. That doesn't seem to be an acceptable solution. But one safeguard would help. I believe that all communications on the Internet should include a name and verifiable e-mail address. That would allow you the ability to find who's sending unwanted material through the Internet to your computer. That way anyone could inform the business or individual to stop. Today, that's almost impossible because many spammers move from one anonymous name to another, much like mailers using a post office box. Such disclosure would allow police authorities the ability to detect any criminal activity with much greater ease than constantly seeking the information from the Internet service providers such as AOL. Finally, it would allow consenting adults to say whatever they want in private chat rooms, but it would make it easier to determine if those individuals are at least eighteen years old.

170

The Government and the Internet: Freedom of the Press, Copyright, Advertising, and Fraud

The Internet is transforming our lives—serving as our new town square, changing the way we live, the way we work, and the way we learn.   —Bill Clinton

On January 21, 1997, President Clinton used the word "Internet" for the first time in a State of the Union address. His speech also happened to be the first such address carried live on the Internet. Despite the Clinton administration's apparent embrace of the information superhighway, what exactly is the government's attitude toward the Internet? Can government tax business transactions on the Internet? Can consumers be protected? What laws exist for journalists? What copyright statutes apply to the Internet?

First and foremost, the president has challenged Americans "to connect every classroom and library in America to the information superhighway by the year 2000 with trained teachers and top quality educational software." The administration has estimated that it will cost $10 billion over the next five years to hook up all of America's public schools. But who's going to pay for universal access? It appears that those who already use the Internet may pay for access for others. Specifically, those with more than one telephone will play an additional fee each year, and the money will be used to finance public schools unable to afford Internet access.

Computer columnist Michael Schrage puts his opposition succinctly: "Just Say No Net in Schools."[1] In the electronic magazine *HotWired*, Schrage maintains the administration plan misses the point. "Clinton's Internet infatuation offers a pathetic but telling symbol of just how much the history and role of technology in education is misunderstood. This infatuation is about politics and pandering, not promise and potential." Schrage argues that Teddy Roosevelt did not and should not have asked for a telephone on every school desk and an operator in every classroom because Alexander Bell's grand invention could change American society. John F. Kennedy, who understood the power of television, should not have put a television set into every classroom, which may have cost more than sending a man to the moon, Schrage argues, adding that the Internet is simply the latest technology that "desperate educators, parents, and politicians" are heralding rather than confronting the need to heighten the quality of teachers and create appropriate curricula. Even Samuel Sava, the head of the National Association of Elementary School Principals, tends to agree with Schrage's assessment. "I have not the slightest doubt about the value of computers in our society," he says. "We must have the courage to resist the public enthusiasm for sexy hardware and argue for the funds necessary to train our teachers."[2]

For example, take a look at the New York City school system. To provide computer access for the city's more than 1,000 public schools will cost an estimated $2 billion for more than 130,000 new computers. "All the money and machines in the world won't mean a damned thing to the city's school children without teachers who know how to turn a mish-mash of bytes into effective teaching tools," maintains technology advocate Tom Watson, the coeditor of industry newsletter @NY. "Too much attention is paid to wires and machines, while too little attention is paid to what can be done with them."[3]

Education represents only one way the Clinton White House wants to present a user-friendly approach to its constituents via the Internet. A federal program, Access America, would bring government services into the digital age by the year 2000. "The idea of reengineering through technology is critical. We didn't want to automate the old, worn processes of government," argues Vice President Al Gore, who has pushed the much-heralded bridge to the twenty-first century. For example, the program would process student loan applications on line, provide Medicare information and payment options for senior citizens, and give businesses export assistance over the Internet.[4] Still, one of the first major experiments at the Social Security Administration was shut down temporarily because of fears that sensitive financial records of millions of Americans may have been at risk. The service allows you to look up earnings and benefit estimate statements after you enter your name, Social Security number, your mother's maiden name, your birthdate, and place of birth. Privacy experts maintained that scam artists, nosy friends, and relatives could gain access to the confidential information.[5]

So far, no Federal *Computer* Commission regulates the Internet. The Federal Communications Commission is about as close to any agency that could govern the Internet, and top policymakers there say they want to leave the Internet alone. Kevin Werbach, the FCC's counsel for new technology policy, argues that the government's role should be to foster technological advancement and widespread public access for the Internet, not to regulate it. "The Internet holds the potential to dramatically change the communications landscape," argues Werbach in "Digital Tornado: The Internet and Telecommunications Policy."[6] A top Clinton White House advisor agrees. "I think the Internet is a medium that will flourish best if it can grow organically," says Ira Magaziner, the former health care crusader who heads government policy on electronic commerce. Magaziner endorses the "anarchy" of the Internet. "The Internet ought to be allowed to take its own directions as much as possible," he says. "I think it's a new medium. I don't think traditional laws are what should apply."

Can government tax business on the Internet? Without question. Nearly $1 billion worth of goods and services was purchased via the Internet in 1996, more than a 60 percent increase over the previous year. That occurred despite concerns many people have about the security of sending credit card information over the Internet.[7] By the year 2000, such sales are expected to quadruple. So what is the federal government going to do? Magaziner wants to prevent federal and state governments from imposing taxes.[8] "In recent years, the Internet has blossomed into an appliance of everyday life, an informational medium accessible from almost every point on the planet. Over the next decade, it will produce profound changes in the prevailing economic order, with the potential to benefit the citizens of all nations," Magaziner argues. The major policy recommendations include no new taxes on the Internet, industry self-regulation where appropriate, and the creation of a uniform commercial code for cyberspace. The plan hopes to provide a "predictable legal environment" for transactions, contracts, liability, privacy, and security.

But more than a few business organizations greet Magaziner's apparent conversion to free-market principles rather skeptically. Remember that Magaziner and First Lady Hillary Clinton headed a plan to increase government regulation and involvement in the health care field. Bill Frezza, a general partner at Adams Capital Management, says he is particularly troubled by one of the "guiding principles" of the administration's policy: regulation should be imposed only as a necessary means to achieve a goal on which broad consensus exists. "This is not a principle," Frezza argues. "This is a political blank check—an invitation to unbridled intervention."[9]

Can consumers be protected on the Internet? Not easily. "It's the Wild, Wild West. You don't really have to worry about truth in advertising. At least not yet," says an advertising expert in New York. This specialist does not intend to take advantage of the loopholes in the system, but there is a great deal of truth in what he says. Standard agreements for print newspapers and classified advertising restrict the type of advertisements accepted for publication. The advertisements face review and established standards. That's not true—at least so far—for the Internet. Fraudulent practices, however, can be prosecuted. The Federal Trade Commission has investigated suspected fraud in cooperation with state officials. The FTC has filed lawsuits to shut down companies running on-line pyramid schemes and bogus adult entertainment sites that cost consumers millions. FTC regulators and attorney generals from twenty-four states found Web sites that promised huge returns on consumer investments. After identifying more than two hundred suspicious sites in April 1997, the FTC sent the marketers warning letters that the businesses must back up their claims or face possible prosecution. More than fifty sites simply closed up shop on the Web, but investigators fear the sites may return. Minnesota authorities have aggressively pursued Internet scams as have Illinois and Georgia. But take a look at this scenario: Items for sale on the Web include homemade jams, movies, books, computers, and magazine subscriptions. What happens when the homemade jam is crawling with microscopic creatures that cause convulsions when combined with butter and English muffins? AOL and other major Internet providers, as well as most newspapers, include clauses in their on-line advertising agreements that the advertisers are responsible for defective and dangerous products. But in this scenario, a man who supplements his Social Security checks makes this special jam. Here the consumer is likely to sue the media outlet that accepted the advertisement and took a commission on the sale.[10] As always, the best advice for consumers may be caveat emptor: buyer beware.

How will government, particularly the courts, treat the rights of digital journalists? Will digital journalists have the same rights as print and television journalists? Perhaps, but it's difficult to tell precisely. Keep in mind, the Internet skirts the globe instantaneously and does not stop at national borders. In Germany, the government indicted the head of CompuServe because users sent pornography through the Internet provider. Moreover, the Germans have made it illegal to discuss on-line topics concerning neo-Nazis, the glorification of Adolf Hitler, and the Third Reich. China requires users and Internet providers to register with the police. In Singapore, political and religious groups must register with the government. In Saudi Arabia, the Internet can only be used at universities and hospitals.

Libel laws are expected to be the same in cyberspace in the United States. *Except*—and it's a big exception—laws in other countries can be significantly different from U.S. law. In Great Britain, for example, the standard argument can be simply stated as "the greater the truth, the greater the libel."[11] American laws define defamation—slander by word of mouth or libel by printed word—as a false statement of fact about an identifiable individual or group that causes injury to one's reputation. To win a lawsuit, a plaintiff must prove that a false statement occurred and caused financial damage. So-called public figures such as politicians must demonstrate that the speaker or publication showed "actual malice" and "recklessly disregarded facts" that were readily available.

The media were not always so well protected. But in the case of New York Times *v. Sullivan*, the rules of defamation dramatically changed. On March 29, 1960, the *New York Times* ran a full-page advertisement entitled, "Heed Their Rising Voices." The advertisement aimed at generating support for the civil rights movement. City Commissioner L. V. Sullivan of Montgomery, Alabama, sued the *New York Times* for being libeled in the advertisement even though he was not named. Some facts in the ad were indeed false. An Alabama jury awarded Sullivan $500,000— generally regarded as an expression of disdain for the northern media—but the U.S. Supreme Court held that a public official could not win a defamation action against the press unless the media acted with "malice." The ruling allowed the media to comment on public affairs without fear of a libel suit even though the report may have been inaccurate. If, however, it could be shown that the publication had violated the higher standard, then a public figure could win a lawsuit.

178

How do these principles affect on-line publications? The basic issue centers on whether the publisher controls the content of the publication. If so, the publisher can be held liable for any statements made in cyberspace. But it's tricky. For example, bookstores and libraries do not have the time to review or the power to change the content of a book or newspaper that may make libelous statements. Therefore, a distributor such as a bookstore generally cannot be sued. But what about discussion groups and chat rooms of on-line publications? Is the publication responsible for what a disgruntled employee says about his or her company in a discussion group? "I have advised clients that chat rooms are fraught with problems. You can't control them. I don't know that there's any legal protection," Washington computer lawyer Neal J. Friedman acknowledges.

Two cases offer some guidance on this issue, although a definitive answer remains elusive. In one case, CompuServe published a newsletter on line. CompuServe hired a company, which signed a contract with a third company, Don Fitzpatrick Associates, to provide news and information about the entertainment business. Fitzpatrick wrote a column, "Rumorville USA," that appeared on CompuServe. In 1990, a company charged that CompuServe had written defamatory comments. A federal court in New York, however, determined that CompuServe had no editorial control over the product and served much like a library or bookstore. Therefore, CompuServe faced no liability.

In the second case, *Stratton Oakmont v. Prodigy*, the courts ruled for Stratton, an investment firm. A former employee made anonymous, but derogatory, comments about Stratton Oakmont in a forum, "Money Talk." Through the 1990s, Prodigy had marketed itself as a family-oriented, on-line service. The company claimed it would prohibit insulting, harassing, and tasteless comments. Prodigy also warned users that posts would be monitored and potentially deleted if improper. Ironically, Prodigy's attempt to keep its site clean meant the company acted as a publisher, and therefore was liable for any remarks made by those using the service.[12]

Other legal anomalies exist for digital journalism. For example, a publisher usually faces a libel suit only within the publication's circulation area. The *Boston Globe*, for example, usually would be sued in Massachusetts or perhaps a few neighboring states. But the *Globe*'s Internet edition can be accessed throughout the world, making it possible to sue the publication in a variety of courts. So far, no court cases have provided guidance on what publishers or users should do. In some states, journalists can refuse to provide government officials with the identity of individuals who provide information to a newspaper. Known as "shield laws," the protections give journalists a special status similar to doctors, lawyers, and the clergy, who can have so-called privileged conversations. For example, if an individual confessed he committed murder to a priest, the police and prosecutors could not force the priest to testify about the information from that privileged conversation. A lawyer cannot be forced to talk about conversations with a client. In some states, journalists cannot be forced to tell the government who provided information for a story. Does the digital journalist have the same protection? Maybe. Again, no legal cases have determined if a digital journalist or the digital media have the same legal protections as other media. David Bartlett, the former president of the Radio-Television News Directors Association, argues that legal protections must extend to digital media. "As the next giant step in communications technology is taken, the First Amendment protections traditionally associated with print journalism . . . must be carried forward and applied to the emerging new media."[13]

180   Another legal question is who actually owns the information in cyberspace? The Internet has been described as the "world's biggest copying machine." With a simple click here and a simple click there, you can obtain reams of data and information. But can you use it outside of your home? Can you publish it on your Web page? Can you send it to your friends? Can you post it on a discussion group? Welcome to the wonderful world of copyright law. The answer right now to all of the questions is you can probably get away with it unless the information comes from a large company with aggressive lawyers.[14] Copyright on the World Wide Web is one of the most contentious Internet issues. Information might be touted as free, but content owners aren't going to keep giving it away for free. "The culture of the Net has always been free exchange of information. But it's not free anymore," says Dan Burk, a professor at Seton Hall University School of Law. "There are big bucks tied up there." The Copyright Act of 1976 grants authors of "original works" the exclusive right to copy and distribute their own work. If another individual or company copies or distributes the work with the creator's permission, the author can seek legal damages in court. Technically, a computer makes a copy of a Web page in order to allow us to read it, which probably violates the letter of existing copyright law. "Old models don't translate well to this medium," Burk says. There are some doctrines that can provide a measure of protection. "Fair use," for example, protects those who copy ma-

terial for educational purposes and not for profit. Here some legal precedents exist. In Playboy *v. Frena*, the magazine claimed that photographs—without the magazine's approval—were copied via computer and put on a bulletin board service in Florida. George Frena, the systems operator of the company, Techs Warehouse, was charged with copyright and trademark infringement. A federal court determined in 1993 that Frena violated *Playboy*'s copyright on the photographs because the magazine gave no approval and received no payment for the material. In a second case, *Sega v. MAPHIA*, a federal court in California closely followed the Frena case. Sega charged that the MAPHIA bulletin board service had copied Sega games without paying for them. But a third case, *Religious Technology Center v. Netcom*, determined that Netcom, an Internet service provider, was not responsible for copyright infringement when the teachings of the Church of Scientology were posted to the site. Ultimately, Netcom settled the matter out of court for an unspecified sum.[15]

A key test of copyright law involved several of the media's heaviest of heavyweights. The *Washington Post*, CNN, and the *Wall Street Journal* filed a lawsuit against a popular Web site, TotalNews, accusing it of illegally republishing and repackaging on-line Web pages for profit.[16] TotalNews, which is based in Phoenix, provides users access to sites operated by many leading news media companies. When these sites appeared on the computer, TotalNews captured the material inside a computer technology known as a "frame." These frames let you read a *Washington Post* article. But the technology kept you on the TotalNews site rather than sending you electronically to the *Washington Post* site, which is customary in similar services. TotalNews president Roman Godzich maintained his company did nothing wrong because the service provided a disclaimer that TotalNews wasn't affiliated with the sites in its directory. But Godzich changed the way viewers used the technology to satisfy the heavyweights he apparently did not want to face in court. Now TotalNews sends the individual to the original site for the report.

News and information on the Web face some significant challenges in the next millennium. The way the government and the courts treated traditional media may apply in some cases to the digital age, but lawyers for new media operations may face not only uncharted, but often hostile, territory.

chapter twelve

The Future of the Internet

Never make forecasts, especially about the future.
—Samuel Goldwyn

As I wandered through the vast blinking, flashing expanse of Internet World in New York's Jacob Javits Convention Center, I could almost imagine that the sorcerer's apprentice had switched from water buckets to silicon chips, unleashing this wild rush of glitzy displays and cockamamie promotional stunts. Dressed like a zebra, twenty-five-year-old Al Lascano was pushing a product called ZooWorks. The program helps users keep track of where they've been on the World Wide Web—a product many people didn't know they really needed. Lascano claimed he would do whatever it took to sell the product, including looking like a zebra. "If the price is right, I'll do anything," Lascano said. "*If* the price is right." Just then, a young woman, dressed in a golden globe wrapped around her torso and a gold crown on her head, walked by. The insignia on the globe read, "Acquion.com," a company that lets you buy almost everything on the Internet, including crude oil. "We want to acquire the world," she cooed. Glitterati meet digerati.

At conventions from Internet World to Comdex, the annual Las Vegas technology summit, the buzzword is content: providing information to consumers on the Internet. But the emphasis of many manufacturers seems to be simply hawking products, not content. Standing in the midst of all this, thoughtful people couldn't help but wonder if the Web's true potential for providing information was being drowned in a rising tide of mindless hype and useless products. At one display at Internet World, an

Israeli company pushed an advertising system to sell automobiles. A viewer could see all sections of the car and zoom into various parts such as the tires and the taillights. But the salesman demonstrating the product was having trouble displaying what his assistant had described as "streaming video." It was not working on one computer, which provided a blurry image. "Are you sure this is streaming video?" I asked. "It looks like a series of digital pictures. Streaming video is different. It means a continuous video picture." The salesmen ignored the question, probably realizing that the product was not what he said it was. But maybe someone else would be a bit more gullible. Nearby, grown men in business suits tossed small basketballs into the air, promoting a product with the slogan, "Nothing But Net." Another new marketer complained to service technicians that the computer connections were not working, and she wanted them fixed *now*.

"Safe systems" has become a mantra almost as commonplace as safe sex. How do you protect a company's information from hackers or convince customers that providing their credit card numbers on the Web is safe? "Encryption" is the buzz word. Convincing advertisers to join the Web is a problem, but myriad, often conflicting solutions exist. New banner advertising. Click-through counters. No banner advertising.

A large computer manufacturer wanted to sell new forms of audio and video connections to businesses. The demonstrator chose an audio program on the Web—accurately described as "streaming audio," which basically means it's available whenever the user wanted to hear it—and clicked on a jazz station. The audio sounded so bad he quickly turned to another station, where the audio was equally poor. The company intended to offer videoconferencing, but what it provided was a herky-jerky, almost unwatchable video program that made black-and-white television look like a major technical innovation. A few systems can offer quality roughly the same as standard television. Unfortunately, the image on a computer measures about two inches square. For anything larger, the programs offer "scanning rates" of about twelve frames per second. A normal television scans at a rate nearly three times faster, meaning the computer version looks like a bad version of a silent film, except in color.

At least IBM Chairman and Chief Executive Officer Louis V. Gerstner, Jr., got it. "A lot of what's gone on in the last twelve months is just plain confusing and exasperating to our customers," he told the conference. "I wouldn't be surprised to see an Internet backlash soon—a 'net weariness' set in. All those end users wondering if this is a waste of time. All those businesses wondering if this is a waste of money." At some point, the technology will work. But it sure doesn't look good now. "I'm so confused about all these solutions," one buyer conceded. "I have to concentrate on only a few. Otherwise, I get lost."

He was not alone. Let me give you a few personal examples of what's going wrong. Bear in mind, I teach this stuff to college students. I am not a computer programmer, but I have been working in this area for a long time. If this rat can't find an occasional and relatively easy way to the cheese, then why should you be expected to do it? The reason that only 10 percent of the American public can program a VCR is because the VCR is a ridiculously complicated piece of junk. It may be your fault you bought the useless piece of junk, but it's not your fault you can't program your VCR. It's the fault of the company that provided you with dozens of pages of complicated instructions, albeit in four languages. Would you accept the same kind of nonsense from your car dealer if your automobile didn't work properly? Of course not. The same standards apply to computer companies and computer programs. Stand up for simplicity. You are the one paying thousands of dollars for this stuff.

In September 1996, I tried to subscribe to an on-line publication. When I tried to access the site, a message informed me that my version of Microsoft's browser would not work properly on the site. I downloaded another version, which took twenty minutes, and tried again. Then the company's computer determined twice that my zip code in the required form that I filled out on-line was wrong; therefore, I could not purchase the publication. I have lived in the same house for nine years, and the zip code hasn't changed. Three days later I was able to subscribe.

At various times, I log on to America Online to evaluate its service. Almost every time I try to test the AOL system, something goes wrong. One time in 1997, the registration did not accept my credit card, and I had to call customer service. I had entered the expiration of my card as 6/98, not 0698. I was on hold for ten minutes before someone told me that. So I filled out the form again and then logged on. After two minutes, I clicked on What's Hot on the Internet. I chose two search engines described by AOL as "great." Then my computer froze. I tried again. I received the message, "We're sorry, but our host computer cannot process your request. There were too many requests pending. Please continue, and try again in a few minutes. If you keep getting this message, please repeat using keyword system response. Thank you." I was wondering how congested the search engines could be. So I went to my usual Internet provider to find out. In less than one minute, I was able to access both sites. A week later, I tried AOL again. Two times, AOL froze my computer screen. The third time, I spent nearly eight minutes on-line to receive the message, "We're sorry, but our host computer cannot process your request." By the summer of 1997, AOL was supposed to be better, so I tried again. When I subscribed to AOL, the electronic form determined that my home address was not valid. So I made one up, which AOL accepted. Then I faced the same delays and frustrations I found earlier.

On the first day of the news merger between NBC News and

Microsoft, I tried to listen to Tom Brokaw's interview with President Clinton. I really tried. I live thirty-five miles north of New York City in Ossining, where MSNBC is not available on my local cable stations. No radio station near my home offers NBC News. So I tried to find Brokaw and Clinton on the MSNBC Internet site. I used a version of Microsoft's own Internet Explorer, and the message read, "This program does not support the protocol." I then tried to access the site with Microsoft's competitor, Netscape. I found an audio clip from an earlier speech by Clinton about welfare reform, which is known as a "loop" in the broadcasting business. An audio loop establishes an active hookup that will change when live programming begins. "We want people to work full time and live in dignity," Clinton said repeatedly. Three times, the loop froze my computer. When I tried to join the Ask Clinton Forum, I needed a password. I could not find any place to obtain a password. I finally gave up and thought I would read the promised transcript the next day. When I tried, the transcript wasn't available.

Then there's *U.S. News & World Report*. At the end of 1996, the magazine offered a series of articles both in print and on-line entitled, "Outlook for 1997: Silver bullet solutions for tough problems." Rather than simply writing about issues, reporters and editors provided solutions to subjects from education to elderly health care. One writer, John Simons, described the Internet as "lurching toward doom" because of serious bandwidth troubles that slowed communication (see chapter 9). When I tried to join the discussion to disagree with some observations in the article, the *U.S. News* Online Chat Board dutifully told me, "Sorry, we could not find the specified comments area. Please select one of the following articles or comment areas." The chat board spewed forth so much material that I finally had to shut off my computer. The information dealt with the magazine's ratings of colleges, not the Internet. (By the way, I always use the rule of threes in testing

Web sites: at least three tries on three different days. I actually tried the site five times and got the same frustrating results.)

My message is simple: The Internet and the World Wide Web have a great deal to offer. Unfortunately, many news and information providers are not using the medium effectively. Not that long ago, the movie *Field of Dreams*, which focused on building a baseball field in the middle of nowhere, gave many Web designers and manufacturers the mantra, "Build it and they will come." Today, the mantra should focus on reality rather than dreams, "Build it well and make it easy. Otherwise, they will not come." When I pick up a telephone, I expect to hear a dial tone. When I click on my remote control, I expect my television to turn on. When I walk out my door at 7:30 A.M., I expect my newspaper to be in the driveway or at least in the rose bushes nearby. Right now, the Internet and the World Wide Web cannot offer the typical user the same reliability of other media. Until digital media can do that, people will not come. If people do not come, advertisers will not come. If advertisers do not come, digital journalism will die.

There has been no dearth of predictions about the future of communications through the years. The telegraph was supposed to end war for all time, based on the belief that if people would communicate their differences instantaneously, there would be no misunderstandings and no need to fight wars. Purportedly, the telephone would destroy the American family, eliminate loneliness, rebuild rural life, make skyscrapers possible, and make the world more democratic.[1] Here are some predictions about the future of news and information on the Internet and the World Wide Web from a variety of analysts:

David Bartlett (former president, Radio and Television News Directors Association)

Consumers will be able to participate in the news process. Journalism will become less of a lecture and more of a conversation. Journalists will spend less time guessing what their customers might want to know and more time packaging and organizing an almost infinite body of raw material into reliable and useful information packages.[2]

190

More separate news organizations will appear, each a good deal smaller and more specialized than those we see today. From these smaller and more efficient news operations, a far greater volume and variety of news will emerge, aimed at much smaller audiences than today's news departments. The very notion of "mass" media will fade into history. Before long, the hot news format will be individually customized "information on demand." News gathering and production equipment will continue to get cheaper and easier to use. The news gathering and presentation process that once required a large staff of technical specialists will be performed quite routinely by lone reporters armed with inexpensive camcorders, notebook computers, and portable telephones. The material these newspersons produce will be simultaneously created and distributed in a wide variety of formats. To survive in this more demanding and competitive environment, news producers will have to find new ways to profit from smaller shares of the total audience.

Dominique Paul Noth (computer consultant and former *Milwaukee Journal* on-line columnist)

We are neglecting what journalists dare not neglect—the dramatic power of telling stories, the need to interpret events, and cast ideas in ways that matter.

We have forgotten that e-mail, home pages, forums, unfolding threads, feuds, freedom of choice, freedom of the road to travel—all these expressions of the human spirit and the need for emotional and intellectual contact—have been core reasons for the bursting Internet.

When floods devastated the Midwest (in 1997), we got weather reports, repurposed headlines of disasters. It was not news sites primarily that provided the human dialog among the victims and the sympathizers. No sites put together in alert, touching journalistic ways the photo of the family and the audio of their disbelief with the meaningfully punctuated chart of how much time and money would be involved in recovery.

The digital age is ripe with tools, and with economies of scale, that open powerful ways of telling stories and interpreting—not merely disgorging—information. What media companies are putting R and D money into this? Which universities? What news providers? A few here and there try, and a few more talk about it. Until more do, on-line news will not fulfill its promise nor will it become vital in feeding the real news hunger of our society and culture.

Clifford Stoll (engineer and author, *Silicon Snake Oil*)

The Internet is a perfect diversion from learning . . . [it] opens many doors that lead to empty rooms. The information highway is being sold to us as delivering information, but what it's really delivering is data. . . . Unlike data, information has utility, timeliness, accuracy, a pedigree. . . . Editors serve as barometers of quality, and most of an editor's time is spent saying no.[3]

John Lancaster (computer consultant)

If we citizens use this opportunity wisely, we can be the best-informed voters in the history of the world. Documentation of legislation—who sponsored it, who voted for or against it, and so on—is literally available to any citizen now. That's a powerful tool for freedom.

Norman Pearlstine (editor-in-chief, *Time* magazine)

From the time of Gutenberg, publishing has been one speaking to the many. The promise of "new media" is a format of many speaking to the many. Communicating with each other also creates a community. The one thing that might create a problem is in the editing community. When you buy the *New York Post* or the *New York Times*, you commit to a predictable quality of information. You understand what you're getting. We're not yet sure of a consistent standard on the Internet.

Howard Rheingold (author, *The Virtual Community*)

Because of its potential influence on so many people's beliefs and perceptions, the future of the Net is connected to the future of community, democracy, education, science, and intellectual life—some of the human institutions people hold most dear, whether or not they know or care about the future of computer technology. The future of the Net has become too important to leave to specialists and special interests . . . We need a clear citizens' vision of the way the Net ought to grow, a firm idea of the kind of media environment we would like to see in the future. If we do not develop such a vision for ourselves, the future will be shaped for us by large commercial and political powerholders.[4]

Stewart Baker (partner, Steptoe and Johnson)

The "free-wheeling, anything-goes attitude" found on much of the World Wide Web could become less prevalent as big business moves in.[5]

Elizabeth Osder (content editor, *New York Times on the Web*)

The Internet is going to be dominated by a few large players. Pathfinder is where people go for everything. MSNBC is where people go for everything. The *New York Times* is where people go for everything.

David Haskin (computer consultant)

The Internet is not a business segment that can easily be dominated. It most assuredly is not just another type of delivery medium, a remarkably efficient digital printing press. Rather, it is a constantly changing, totally participatory, freelance democracy that will be impossible to "control," at least for many years. Even Bill Gates isn't trying to control it, he's merely trying to control all the software that's used for it. The barriers to entry into this world are minimal—if you know how to create a Web page (something even nontechnical people can do), you can be a journalist. That, of course, is good news for democracy and for the decentralization of the news gathering process. But it's not necessarily good news for the news business.

News organizations that don't understand these fundamental

differences with the "old" world will not succeed on the Net. Put differently, news gathering and dissemination is a brand new ballgame now, not just a variation of the old way of doing things.

Robert Metcalfe (computer systems developer)

Users of news and information won't change except there will be more of them. On-line will be when you want it and searchable. Telephone, TV, and on-line will converge slowly. There will be many more journalists and much more news. Verifying facts and sources will be harder on-line—a new responsibility for journalists.

Tom Phillips (president, ABC Internet Ventures)

Newspapers are the most threatened because their revenue source is the most threatened. Fifty percent of their revenue should go to nearly zero in the next ten years, maybe in five. . . . People will still want the daily newspaper delivered ten years from now. But that daily newspaper can't afford to deliver it to me.

Jay Small (editor, *Indianapolis Star-News Online*)

Print will be dominant for the foreseeable future, at least ten years, because:

> It's still easier to read, carry, and dispose of.
>
> It's still cheaper for most people.
>
> It's still more accessible.

Newspaper companies are not yet ready to shift large percentages of their resources to any other medium. By sheer momentum (or lack thereof), those companies can keep interest in print high, for a while, at least.

A new medium can and probably will overtake print when it exists in at least one room of almost every home and business, like TV or the telephone. Its commonplace existence makes the addition of newspaper delivery via this new medium a small extra expense. It is as easy or easier to read and use, and offers values of scale and quality that are not possible in print.

Good reporters will still have a role. Good editors will still have a role. Good technologists will be a dime a dozen.

195

Robert Pittman (chief executive officer, American Online)

I don't think content in this business is what it is in the television business. At AOL, we're giving people convenience in a box. People don't need to know more about the news or more about their computer; they don't need more places to talk to people. What they need are more convenient activities. And what's winning here is content that is more convenient. What we're about is [this]: If I like to go out to bars just to talk to people and drink a couple of beers, I [could also] go to a chat room. That's more convenient than going out to the bar. If I'm a kid and I've got to do a term paper, instead of going to the library I go search the Internet for my subject. That's a lot more convenient.[6]

George Gilder (author, *Life After Television*)

The new system will be the telecomputer, or "teleputer," a personal computer adapted for video processing and connected by fiber-optic threads to other teleputers all around the world. Using a two-way system of signals like telephones do, rather than broadcasting one-way like TV, the teleputer will surpass the television in video communication just as the telephone surpassed the telegraph in verbal communication. . . . Television is a tool of tyrants. Its overthrow will be a major force for freedom and individuality, culture, and morality. That overthrow is at hand.[7]

Peter Jennings (ABC News anchor)

ABCnews.com (the ABC News Web site) is very good for ABC radio and television because it is such a good product that it will help to reemphasize in the public's mind that this is a serious news organization that provides context and depth.

The attraction of the Internet is not being absorbed by very many people. I don't think of the Internet as an outright competitor with the evening news. Maybe that will change in the future, but not just yet.

Robert Stearns (vice president for corporate development, Compaq)

We're involved in developing room-based devices that look very different from today's boxes on the desk. They will hang on the wall, be more intuitive, and have interaction styles tailored for various members of the family.[8]

Paul Saffo (director of the Institute for the Future)

We talk about the personal computer as revolutionary. It may well be, someday, but it has hardly been revolutionary yet compared to other innovations. . . . The average consumer video camera has more processing power on board than the top-of-the-line (late 1980s PC) did in its heyday. . . . Why should I care that my camera has that processing power? It allows me to take very good pictures in extremely low light. Which is why you have a videotape by an ordinary citizen of the police beating of Rodney King. That's a real revolution. So we will look back thirty years from now, and we're going to say the personal computer was very interesting, but it was the horseless carriage of this whole thing. The real revolution's going to be working in devices that people hardly notice.[9]

Eric K. Meyer (on-line consultant and educator)

Bandwidth will increase while costs decrease? Expect one or the other but not both. The dominant audience is composed of voracious readers who seek out the Net as a source of augmentation for other material already available to them in traditional forms.[10]

Robert Denny (software developer)

There will be a big shakeout among Internet service providers. Those that will survive will fall into two categories: either they will be among the largest or they will have value-added services that are reliable and cheap. . . . Getting on the Internet will remain cheap, getting down to the bare-metal pricing—and it will be flat-rate. But Microsoft will reveal plans to buck the Internet flat-rate trend with some form of usage-based pricing for its products.

Kirkpatrick Sale (leader of the Neo-Luddites)

I was on the stage of New York City's Town Hall with an audience of 1,500 people. I was behind a lectern, and in front of the lectern was this computer. And I gave a very short, minute-and-a-half description of what was wrong with the technosphere, how it was destroying the biosphere. And then I walked over and I got this very powerful sledgehammer and smashed the screen with one blow and smashed the keyboard with another blow. It felt wonderful. The sound it made, the spewing of the undoubtedly poisonous insides into the spotlight, the dust that hung in the air ... some in the audience applauded.[11]

John Gage (chief scientist, Sun Microsystems)

198   The application of Internet connectivity is not just about putting up Web pages of today's news, but about altering how things work. We've only made computers smaller, lighter, and more powerful. Everything we're doing now is wrong. Complexity is death.[12]

Nicholas Negroponte (founder of the MIT Media Lab and author, *Being Digital*)

The rate of change is what's mind-boggling. Even the people who were considered way out on the far left, like myself ... really underestimated this one. We badly undershot. Let me give you [a] very precise [example]: Both Apple Computer and IBM, whether or not they will agree that this is correct, really did not think of the home as a market as recently as four years ago, maybe five. . . . It's happened so rapidly and so recently that even the founders of the Internet, people who were very much aware of the potential, would never have guessed this rate of change.[13]

Vinton G. Cerf (senior vice president, MCI Telecommunications)

It's risky to predict the future of something as dynamic as the Internet. It seems safe to say that we will see a continuing explosion of new services. . . . There is every reason to believe that the Internet will transform education, business, government, and personal activities in ways we cannot fully fathom. Virtually none of this would have happened as rapidly, or in the same open and inclusive fashion, had not the federal government consciously provided sustained research funding and encouragement of open involvement and open standards, and then wisely stepped out of the picture as the resulting systems became self-sustaining. The Internet is truly a global infrastructure for the twenty-first century—the first really new infrastructure to develop in nearly a century.[14]

Bill Gates (Microsoft)

The information highway will transform our culture as dramatically as Gutenberg's press did the Middle Ages. When tomorrow's powerful machines are connected on the highway, people, machines, entertainment, and information services will all be accessible.[15]

Johann Gutenberg apparently had little difficulty determining what book he would publish when he invented the printing press in the middle of the fifteenth century: the Bible. The printing of the Bible made it available to the public—a factor that many believe laid the foundation for the upheaval in organized religion. Individuals could now read the Bible without any interpretation from the clergy, and they didn't like what the priests were doing with church doctrine and religious practices. Without Gutenberg's Bible, it is unlikely that Martin Luther would have received widespread public support after he pinned his complaints about the Roman Catholic Church on the door of the Wittenberg church, starting the Protestant Reformation in the sixteenth century.

Today, the body politic again can access news and information without the interpretation of intermediaries. Despite the amount of information that's available now it is somewhat ironic that one book that remains a leading seller: the Bible. Moreover, one of the most frequently visited sites on the World Wide Web is www.vatican.va, the address of the Roman Catholic Church. It is unclear whether the computer and the Internet will have the revolutionary impact of the printing press. Certainly, there are a whole host of issues that must be resolved from bandwidth to bare breasts. But this new medium does provide the opportunity for far more people to access and use the information that exists in the world.

News and Information on the Internet: A Short History

1969

The Defense Department's Advance Research Projects commissions ARPANET to create a computer network, which lays the ground work for the Internet.

1971

Bolt, Beranek, and Newman invents an electronic mail program to send messages across a computer network.

1981

BITNET, the "Because It's Time NETwork," is launched as a cooperative network at the City University of New York with the first connection to Yale. The service provides electronic mail, listserv servers to distribute information, and file transfers.

1982

The *Fort Worth Star-Telegram*'s StarText opens the first news-paper on-line service, a dial-in bulletin board service. The BBS moves to the Web in 1995.

1983

The Internet begins operation based on the foundation of the ARPANET.

1984

Knight-Ridder opens Viewtron, a news and information serv-ice similar to many of today's on-line sites.

1987

Knight-Ridder shuts down Viewtron after losing $50 million.

1991

American Online goes public, offering news and information services for a fee.
Scientist Timothy Berners-Lee releases the computer program for the World Wide Web.

1992

Knight-Ridder Newspapers opens the Information Design Laboratory in Boulder, Colorado, to design the newspaper of the future.

1993

Wired, the self-proclaimed voice of the digital age, publishes its first edition, and launches *HotWired*, an on-line publication, the next year.

1994

January: About twenty newspaper on-line services are available worldwide, mostly bulletin board services.

NandO, the on-line service of the *Raleigh* (North Carolina) *News and Observer*, launches its service.

Time Inc. starts Pathfinder, its Web site for a variety of publications. Within three years, Pathfinder has four different leaders and is losing $10 million a year.

L'Unione Sarda, a newspaper in Sardinia, goes on-line as the first European newspaper on the Internet.

The *Weekend Independent*, a student newspaper at the University of Queensland in Brisbane, Australia, is that continent's first on-line publication.

The *Weekly Mail and Guardian* in Johannesburg, South Africa, which went on-line in late 1993 as an electronic mail edition, opens its site to become the first African publication on the Web.

December: About a hundred newspaper services operating or under development, including on-line editions on Prodigy of the *Atlanta Journal-Constitution* and the *Los Angeles Times*.

America Online reaches one million subscribers.

1995

February: The *Age* in Melbourne, becomes Australia's first on-line daily publication.

Jornal do Brasil Online becomes South America's first daily publication on the Web. A few days later, Agencia Estado, a Brazilian news agency, launches its Web site.

April: *USA Today* launches its newspaper on-line. At first, the newspaper charges for the service through CompuServe but shortly turns it into a free publication.

Former *Village Voice* reporter Joe Shea launches the *American Reporter*, the first publication with only on-line content.

July: Time magazine runs a cover story on pornography on the Internet entitled, "Cyberporn." The story, which was based on a study at Carnegie Mellon University, turned out to have vastly overestimated the amount of pornography on the Internet.

Knight-Ridder Newspapers closes its new media research center, the Information Design Laboratory.

August: CNN launched its first Web site, *CNN Interactive,* a twenty-four-hour-a-day service.

Steve Outing launches his column, "Stop The Presses," in *Editor & Publisher Interactive.*

September: The *New York Times* and the *Washington Post* publish the 35,000-word manifesto written by the Unabomber. The online edition of the *Post* also publishes the tract, and a few weeks later his brother reads the treatise and alerts authorities.

October: The Times Mirror Center for The People and The Press releases its survey on on-line use. The report finds that the number of Americans going on-line to an information service or directly to the Internet has more than doubled in less than a year to about twelve million.

The *Boston Globe* launches *Boston.com,* which also includes television and radio stations, other local print publications, and a variety of businesses, libraries, community organizations, and museums.

December: Nearly 700 newspapers are operating on-line editions worldwide, an increase from 100 the previous year.

1996

January: The *New York Times* launches its own on-line version on the Web.

American Online reaches five million subscribers.

President Bill Clinton signs into law the Communications Decency Act, which aims at regulating pornography on the Internet. The law is immediately challenged in court as unconstitutional.

Mainichi Shimbun, the third-largest newspaper in Japan, becomes the first publisher to distribute daily editions designed for reading on a portable electronic display, a handheld device called Zaurus.

March: The *Chicago Tribune* launches its own on-line version on the Web.

April: The *Los Angeles Times* relaunches its on-line version on the Web even though an earlier version failed to meet expectations.

The *Wall Street Journal Interactive Edition* goes on-line and starts charging for subscriptions in September.

May: The *Washington Post's Digital Ink* launches its independent Web site.

June: Michael Kinsley, long-time Washington pundit, opens *Slate*, an electronic magazine backed by Microsoft.

The *Minneapolis Star Tribune* opens its full Web site after partial versions that included its series, "On the Edge of the Digital Age," and major daily stories.

July: Microsoft and NBC announce a $440 million joint venture to launch a cable television channel and an accompanying Web service, MSNBC.

August: America Online faces a nineteen-hour blackout that leaves millions of customers without Internet access and disrupts the on-line publications of the *Chicago Tribune* and the *New York Times*.

On its Web site, the *San Jose Mercury News* publishes "Dark Alliance," a series on alleged ties between the CIA and the sale of cocaine in Los Angeles. The series had run earlier in the printed publication. The articles create a clamor among minority groups for an investigation of the allegations.

November: Hackers attack the *New York Times on the Web*

during election night coverage. The news service slows down, but the attack fails. Television viewership of the results drop to an all-time low, while one in ten voters say they visited a Web site concerning politics during the campaign.

Pierre Salinger, former chief European correspondent for ABC News, reported the U.S. Navy accidentally fired a missile that brought down TWA 800 in July 1996, which crashed off Long Island and killed more than 200 people. Salinger cited French security sources for his story, which made headlines throughout the world. A document posted anonymously on the Internet later surfaced as the primary source for the story. The document had been discounted by many other journalists.

December: More than 1,600 newspapers operate on-line editions, including nearly every major newspaper in North America and Europe. That compares with 700 on-line editions the previous year.

AOL launches its service at a fixed monthly price, and users jam the system while some people are left without access.

1997

March: The *Dallas Morning News* reports that Oklahoma City bombing suspect Timothy McVeigh had confessed to the attack to his attorneys. The article appeared first in the publication's on-line edition because the editors decided not to wait for the printed version of the newspaper to provide the information.

Politics Now, generally considered the most popular Web site devoted to American politics, ceases publication apparently as a result of a conflict among the partners, the *National Journal,* the *Washington Post,* and ABC News.

April: Microsoft launches *Sidewalk Seattle,* the first of its on-line information services for cities.

May: ABC News combines with Starwave to offer *ABC.com*, a news service on the Web.

The *San Jose Mercury News* apologizes to its readers for significant errors made in the series "Dark Alliance" about allegations of CIA involvement in Los Angeles drug trafficking.

June: In a 7–2 decision, the U.S. Supreme Court finds unconstitutional the Communications Decency Act, which was intended to restrict pornography on the Internet.

207

Talking Geek: Terms of Internet Endearment

The world of the Internet has a language of its own. Here's some of the lingo. (Sources: "Web Info Internet Glossary"; Krol, *The Whole Internet*; Lemay, *Teach Yourself Web Publishing*; Phil, *Netscape Navigator 2.0*, University of Washington Libraries, "The Internet.")

The Internet

The Internet is an international network of computers ranging from individual personal computers to supercomputers. A wide variety of information is available on the Internet, such as library catalogues, databases, computer files, and discussion groups. The World Wide Web is part of the Internet, and the two words should not be used interchangably, although they often are.

Bookmarks

A function of the browser that allows you to keep a list of interesting sites so they may be easily found again. You often have too many of them. Keep in mind that you can create subject file folders for your bookmarks. That makes it a lot easier than scrolling down a list of dozens of bookmarks. You also can edit the names of bookmarks, so you can bypass the gibberish most of the them include.

Browser

A program that translates and displays information from the World Wide Web. The browser also organizes e-mail and can help you create your own Web pages. Internet Explorer and Netscape are examples of browsers.

Bug

A conflict between various computer programs or a specific problem with your computer. The name derives from an incident when a Defense Department computer maven removed a moth from his system.

Cache

Pronounced "cash." A location in memory where data are stored for easy retrieval.

Client

A software application that works on your behalf to get information from a server somewhere on the network.

Download

The process of transferring computer files to your computer or floppy disk from another computer.

Emoticons

Since people may not understand when you are being ironic, nasty, or nice, a series of emotional scripting devices have developed. These include

:-) or :)	a smiling face
;-) or ;)	a winking, smiling face
:-(or :(	an unhappy face, or "unsmiley"
:-P	someone sticking out his or her tongue
>:-O	someone screaming in fright with his or her hair standing on end
:-&	someone whose lips are sealed

E-mail

Stands for "electronic mail." E-mail is a way to send messages electronically over a computer network.

FAQ

FAQs are documents that list Frequently Asked Questions and their answers.

Error Messages

Error messages may result from a variety of problems. The computer program tries to evaluate a problem and provide you with information to help you solve or get around the problem.

The most common error messages result from trying to bring up a page that is not currently available. The server issuing the page may be temporarily shut down or too busy with other connections to handle your request. You could try the site again at a later time. In addition, the page may no longer exist or it may have a new address. There are a lot of dead ends on the World Wide Web these days, so get used to it.

FTP (File Transfer Protocol)

An Internet tool that allows you to transfer files between two computers connected to the Internet. Anonymous FTP allows you to connect to remote computers and to transfer publicly available computer files without setting up an account and a password. FTPs are often used with government sites and can help you download vast amounts of textual data often much faster than doing it from a Web site.

Gateway

A computer system that transfers data between normally in-compatible applications or networks. It reformats the data so that they are acceptable for the new network or application.

Gopher

Gopher means to find information the Internet. Gophers link you to electronic books, library catalogues, and specialized databases. Developed at the University of Minnesota, where the mascot is a gopher, the searching tool is being replaced more and more by Web sites.

Home Page

This is the introductory page for a World Wide Web site. It provides an introduction to the site, along with hypertext links.

Hypertext

Hypertext organizes information. Highlighted words in a text can be selected to move to another part of the text with related information.

Link

In hypertext documents, the connection from one document to another.

Listserv

An electronic discussion group. There are thousands of list-servs on a variety of topics, which you can join through an e-mail account.

Modem

Equipment that connects a computer to a data transmission line (usually a telephone line). Modem actually comes from "MOdulator-DEModulator."

Netiquette

Informal rules of conduct on the Internet.

Protocol

Protocol is a definition for how computers will act when communicating with each other. Standard protocols allow computers from different manufacturers to communicate and use different software, providing that the programs running on both ends agree on what the data mean.

Server

Software that allows a computer to offer a service to another computer. The computer on which the server software runs.

Surfing

A term that should never have been applied to the Internet. If you surf, you will drown. If you have an idea and a plan to find some information, you will not drown. You will learn.

Usenet

> A network providing access to electronic discussion groups (newsgroups). There are thousands of newsgroups on all subjects, which you can join by using a newsreader program.

URL (Uniform Resource Locator)

> URL is server and path information that locates a document. The URL follows this format: scheme://host-domain[:port]/path/filename. For example, http://www.edu/ithaca.harper/car.html (that's my syllabus for computer-assisted reporting).

World Wide Web (WWW)

> WWW is a hypertext system that provides access to the Internet through programs called network information browsers.

Notes

Notes to Chapter One

1. Henry K. Lee. "Cronkite Pans TV News at Caen Lecture; He Says Internet Presents Society 'Frightful Danger.'" *San Francisco Chronicle.* 13 November 1996, sec. A.

2. W. Russell Neuman. *The Future of Mass Audience.* New York: Cambridge University Press, 1995.

3. Roger F. Fidler. *Mediamorphosis: Understanding New Media.* Thousand Oaks, Calif.: Pine Forge Press, 1997. 53.

4. Vannevar Bush. "As We May Think." *Atlantic Monthly.* July 1995. http://www.isg.sfu.ca/~duchier/misc/vbush.

Notes to Chapter Two

1. National Science Foundation poll April 1997. The survey was based on telephone interviews with 744 students in grades seven through twelve. Margin of error: 4 percent.

2. "Generation X Examined in Major Study: Media Habits, Beliefs about Morality, Religion, Work, Technology Revealed." American Society of Newspaper Editors. (database on-line) 14 August 1996. available from http://www.anse.org.

3. "Cyberspace Survey Shows Generation X Getting Politically Active." Tripod. (database on-line) 22 April 1996. available from http://www.tripod.com.

4. B. G. Yovovich. "Democraphics of Web Use." *Editor & Publisher Interactive.* 25 April 1997. http://www.medinfo.com.

5. John Consoli. "Who's Using the Web? FIND/SVP Survey Results Revealed." *Editor & Publisher Interactive.* 1 August 1997. http://www.medinfo.com.

6. "One in Ten Voters Online for Campaign." Pew Research Center for the People & the Press. (database on-line) 1996. available from http://www.people-press.org/97medmor.htm.

The data include a demographic profile of on-line users:

	% of Total Population	% of On-line Population
Gender		
Male	48	58
Female	52	42
Race		
White	85	86
Nonwhite	14	14
Black	10	9
Age		
18–24	12	23
25–29	10	14
30–49	42	51
50+	35	11
Income		
$75,000+	10	19
$50,000–$74,999	12	19
$30,000–$49,999	25	28
$20,000–$29,999	17	12
Less than $20,000	23	13
Education		
College grad	21	39
Some college	23	30
High school or less	56	30
Region		
East	20	23
Midwest	25	20
South	34	32
West	21	25
Community size		
Large city	20	22
Suburb	23	31
Small city/town	35	32
Rural	21	14

Based on 4.475 interviews/1.082 on-line users.

7. Politically, on-line users tend to be slightly more Republican than the public at large.

8. "One in Ten Voters Online." Pew.

9. "Current Trends in Public Opinion." *Wirthlin Report*. 6, August 1996. 1–4.

10. Everett Rogers. *Communication Technology*. New York: Free Press, 1986. The adoption rate of between 10 and 25 percent of the total potential market remains crucial in what is known as "the diffusion theory," which is based on the work of Professor Rogers of Stanford University. The theory contends that once a technology has diffused into a segment of 10 to 25 percent, the rate of growth will increase dramatically. These patterns have held true for the adoption of radio and television.

11. Ibid. 50.

12. Neuman. *Future of Mass Audience*. 90.

13. "One in Ten Voters Online." Pew.

14. Radio and Television News Directors Foundation (RTNDA). "Profile of the American News Consumer." RTDNA. 1996. 6.

15. Ibid. 24–25.

16. "One in Ten Voters Online." Pew.

17. David Broder. interview by Steve Talbot. Public Broadcasting System. 11 July 1996.

18. Bob Woodward. interview by Steve Talbot. Public Broadcasting System. 29 July 1996.

19. "One in Ten Voters Online." Pew.

20. "TIME/CNN Poll." (database on-line) October 1996. available from http://pathfinder.com.

21. Andrew Heyward. "Keynote Address." Edward R. Murrow Awards. RTNDA. 9 October 1996.

Notes to Chapter Three

1. Brent Schlender. "What Bill Gates Really Wants." *Fortune*. 16 January 1995. http://pathfinder.com.

2. Bill Gates. "Predictions for 1997." *New York Times Special Features*. 30 December 1996. http://www.ntysin.com/live/Latest.

3. Bill Gates. "TV and PC Will Merge in the Age of the Internet." *New York Times Special Features*. 11 April 1996. http://www.ntysin.com/live/Latest.

4. Schlender. "Bill Gates."

5. James Gleick. *Slate*. (database on-line) available from http://www.slate.com.

6. Schlender. "Bill Gates." 34.

7. Todd Savage. "Print Execs, Citizen Gates Squabble at Confab." *Wired Online*. 30 April 1997. http://www.wired.com.

8. Jeff Goodell. "The Fevered Rise of America Online." *Rolling Stone*. 3 October 1996. 60.

9. *Qiews*. December 1996. 293.

10. Goodell. "America Online." 61.

11. *Wired*. December 1996. 256.

12. Anne Lamott. "AOL: Agent of Lucifer." *Salon*. 5 August 1996. http://www.salonmagazine.com/weekly/lamott960805.html.

13. Leah Gentry. "Buckbobill: Journalist." Newspaper Association of America. December 1996. http://www.naa.org.

14. Pamela Shoemaker. *Gatekeeping*. Newbury Park, N.J.: Sage Publications, 1991.

15. Ibid. 46.

16. Ibid. 11.

17. Ibid. 52.

Notes to Chapter Four

1. Adam Clayton Powell III. "Findings from The Freedom Forum's Digital Democracy Project." Freedom Forum. October 1996. http://www.freedomforum.org.

2. The Pew Research Center for the People & the Press. "Diana's Death Interested Everyone." September 1997. http://www.people-press.org.

3. Bruno Giussani. "Mourning Diana: Online Chat Becomes a Book of Condolences." *New York Times on the Web*. 2 September 1997. http://www.nytimes.com.

4. Karla Aronson, George Sylvie, and Russell Todd. "Real-time Journalism." *Newspaper Research Journal*. summer/fall 1996. 53–67.

5. Ibid. 65.

Notes to Chapter Five

1. Eric Meyer. "Online Publishing Continues to Grow Rapidly." *American Journalism Review Online*. April 1997. http://www.newslink.org.

2. Jane Singer. "Changes and Consistencies: Newspaper Journalists Contemplate an Online Future." paper delivered at the Association for Education in Journalism and Mass Communication. August 1996.

3. Matthew Purdy. "The Eureka Search." *New York Times*. 15 December 1996. sec. A.

4. National Transportation Safety Board.

5. Christopher Noble. "Salinger Claims 'Proof' on TWA Missile Theory." *Reuters*. 13 March 1997.

Notes to Chapter Six

1. Joel Brinkley. "Who Will Build Your Next Television?" *New York Times Interactive Edition*. 28 March 1997. http://www.nytimes.com.

2. Karen Huus. "Indonesia." *MSNBC Online*. http://www.msnbc.com.

3. Lee Fleming. "Web Broadcasting: An Overview." Gartner Group. http://gartner4.atvantage.com.

Notes to Chapter Seven

1. "The Web in Perspective: A Comprehensive Analysis of Ad Response." I/Pro. 8 October 1996. http://www.ipro.com.

2. Andrew Sorkin. "Ad Revenue on Web Rises in First Six Months of 1997." *New York Times Interactive Edition*. 4 August 1997. http://www.nytimes.com.

3. Bill Bass and Sara Eichler. "Content Profit Models." Forrester Research. 1 May 1996. (database on-line) available from http://www.forrester.com.

4. AT&T/Odyssey. "Taking Off: The State of Electronic Commerce in America." fall 1996. http://www.att.com.

5. Hoag Levins. "The Online Classified Reports New Cyberspace Advertising Technologies to Impact Newspaper Revenues in 3 Years." *Editor & Publisher Interactive*. 21 November 1996. http://www.mediainfo.com.

Notes to Chapter Eight

1. Thomas K. Glennan and Arthur Melmed. "Fostering the Use of Educational Technology: Elements of a National Strategy." (database on-line) 1996. available from http://www.rand.org.

2. Ibid.

3. Sheila Heaviside, Toija Riggins, and Elizabeth Farris. "Advanced Telecommunications in U.S. Public Elementary and Secondary Schools." National Center for Education Statistics. February 1997.

4. Ibid. In September 1996, questionnaires were mailed to the principals in the 1,000 sampled schools. The principal was asked to forward the questionnaire to the computer or technology coordinator or to whomever was most knowledgeable about the availability and use of advanced telecommunications at the school. A total of 911 schools completed the survey.

5. "Current Trends." *Wirthlin Report.* August 1996. 1–4.

6. The data come from two Wirthlin surveys in August and October 1996. The sample size was 2,009 people.

7. John Markoff. "As Technology Spreads Rural Areas Are Not Being Left Out, Study Finds." *New York Times on the Web.* 24 February 1997. http://www.nytimes.com.

8. "The Consumer Online Usage Study." Simmons Market Research Bureau. (database on-line) March 1997. available at http://www.marketsresearch.com/index.htm.

9. Mike Antonucci. "Age, More Than Income, May Actually Divide the 'Haves' from the 'Have-Nots' in the Digital Age." *San Jose Mercury News Online Edition.* 2 March 1997. http://www.sjmercury.com.

10. William Wresch. *Disconnected.* Brunswick, N.J.: Rutgers University Press, 1996.

11. "Gates Predicts a Wired Africa." *Reuters.* 6 March 1997.

Notes to Chapter Nine

1. "Four Horsemen of Net Apocalypse." *CNET.* 31 October 1996. http://www.news.com.

2. Robert Calem. "Hackers Vandalize C.I.A.'s Web Page." *New York Times on the Web.* 19 September 1996. http://www.nytimes.com.

3. Todd Krieger. "Hackers Go on TV to Show Perils in ActiveX." *New York Times on the Web.* 13 February 1997. http://www.nytimes.com.

4. Judy Holland. "Computer Hackers Clog Capitol Hill." *Hearst Newspapers.* 20 February 1997.

5. *Reuters.* 24 December 1996.

6. Mike Ricciuti. "Hacking Cost Businesses $800 Million." *CNET.* 6 June 1996. http://www.news.com.

7. *BNA Daily Report for Executives.* 6 January 1997. sec. A.

8. "Traffic on the Internet: A Graphic Glossary." *New York Times on the Web.* http://www.nytimes.com.

9. *CNET.* "Four Horsemen."

10. Rob Wells. "IRS: No Handle on Year 2000 Problem." *Associated Press.* 2 April 1997.

11. John Broder and Laurence Zuckerman. "Computers Remain Unready for the Future." *New York Times on the Web.* 7 April 1997. http://www.nytimes.com.

12. Lee Gomes. "A Look at Allstate Shows Why Preparing for 2000 Is So Tough." *Wall Street Journal Interactive Edition.* 9 December 1996. http://www.wsj.com.

Notes to Chapter Ten

1. Todd Richissin. "Sharon Lopatka Anonymously Catered to the Sexual Desires of Others over the Internet." *News & Observer.* 3 November 1996. sec. A.

2. Nina Bernstein. "On Minnesota Prison Computer. Files To Make Parents Shiver." *New York Times on the Web.* 18 November 1996. http://www.nytimes.com.

3. Steve Russell and Joe Shea. *"American Reporter* Challenges CDA." *American Reporter.* 8 February 1996. http://www.newshare.com:9999.

4. John Heilemann. "CDA Update." *HotWired.* 20 March 1997. http://www.hotwired.com.

5. Seth Schiesel. "How Internet Smut Is Regulated May Depend on Tools to Filter It." *New York Times on the Web.* 24 March 1997. http://www.nytimes.com.

6. Brock Meeks. *MSNBC Online.* 25 April 1997. http://www.msnbc.com.

7. "Shielding Your Kids." *Consumer Reports.* May 1997. 30.

8. Calvin Woodward. "Web Filters Are Kind of Erratic." *Associated Press.* 27 March 1997.

9. Charles M. Madigan and Bob Secter. "Second Thoughts on Free Speech." *Chicago Tribune.* 4 July 1997. http://www.chicago.tribune.com.

10. Pamela Mendels. "Court Says Oklahoma University Can Restrict Internet Access." *New York Times on the Web.* 29 January 1997. http://www.nytimes.com.

11. Pamela Mendels. "Censoring Web Sites Poses Dilemma for Librarians." *New York Times on the Web*. 9 March 1997. http://www.nytimes.com.

12. Ashley Craddock. "Texas ISPs Targeted in Secessionist Case." *CNET*. 11 April 1997. http://www.news.com.

13. Janet Kornblum. "ISP Battles for Rebels' Rights." *CNET*. 2 May 1997. http://www.news.com.

14. Jonathan Gaw. "Internet Snoops." *Minneapolis Star Tribune*. 21 March 1996. sec. A.

15. Bill Gates. "The Online Challenge to Individual Privacy." *New York Times Syndicate*. 5 November 1996. http://www.ntysin.com/live/Latest.

Notes to Chapter Eleven

1. Michael Schrage. "Just Say No Net in Schools." *HotWired*. 18 February 1997. http://www.hotwired.com.

2. "Educator Questions Computers' Educational Value." *USA Today*. 17 July 1997. 25.

3. Tom Watson. "A City Plan to Wire Schools." *@NY*. 11 July 1997. http://www.news-ny.com.

4. Courtney Macavinta. "Government Services on the Net." *CNET*. 11 February 1997. http://www.news.com.

5. "Social Security Administration Shuts Down Web Site." *Reuters*. 9 April 1997.

6. Kevin Werbach. "Digital Tornado: The Internet and Telecommunications Policy." FCC. 27 March 1997. http://www.fcc.gov.

7. "The Electronic Marketplace 1997: Strategies For Connecting Buyers & Sellers." Cowles/Simba Research. (database on-line) available from http://www.simbanet.com.

8. Magaziner headed a task force of the Departments of Treasury, State, Justice, and Commerce, as well as the Executive Office of the President, the Council of Economic Advisors, the National Economic Council, the National Security Council, the Office of Management and Budget, the Office of Science and Technology Policy, the Office of the Vice President, and the U.S. Trade Representative. Independent commissions included the Federal Communications Commission and the Federal Trade Commission.

9. Bill Frezza. "Beware of Geeks Bearing Gifts, Ira Magaziner's Principles." *Communications Week.* 14 July 1997. 51.

10. Katherine White and Sam Byassee. "Protecting the Franchise: Legal Issues for Electronic Newspapers." paper presented at Connection '96. 14 June 1996.

11. Ibid.

12. Eric Schlacher and Colley Godward. "System Operator Liability." *Boardwatch.* April 1997. 66–71.

13. David Bartlett. "The Soul of a News Machine: Electronic Journalism in the Twenty-First Century." *Federal Communications Law Journal.* 1994. http://www.law.indiana.edu/fclj/fclj.html.

14. Lauren Gibbons Paul. "It's the World's Biggest Copy Machine." *CNET.* 27 January 1997. http://www.news.com.

15. Schlachter and Godward. "Liability." 66.

16. "News Companies Sue TotalNews For 'Framing' Their Web Sites." *Wall Street Journal Interactive Edition.* 24 February 1997. http:// www/wsj.com.

Notes to Chapter Twelve

1. Neumann. *Future of Mass Audience.* 16.

2. Bartlett. "Soul of a News Machine."

3. Clifford Stoll. *Silicon Snake Oil.* New York: Anchor Books, 1996.

4. Howard Rheingold. *The Virtual Community.* New York: Harper-Perennial Library, 1994.

5. Elizabeth Corcoran. "On the Internet, a Worldwide Information Explosion Beyond Words." *Washington Post.* 30 June 1996. sec. A.

6. Janet Kornblum. "Interview with Robert Pittman." *CNET.* 28 April 1997. http://www.news.com.

7. George Gilder. *Life after Television.* New York: W. W. Norton, 1995.

8. David Kirkpatrick. "Fast Times at Compaq." *Fortune.* 1 April 1996. www.pathfinder.com.

9. Pete Leyden. "Dawn of a New Renaissance." *Minneapolis Star Tribune.* 4 June 1995. sec. A.

10. Eric Meyer. "Predictions for 1997." *American Journalism Review Online.* January 1997. http://www.newslink.org.

11. Kevin Kelley. "Interview with a Luddite." *Wired.* June 1995. http:/ /www.wired.com.

12. Carol Levin and Angela Hickman. "Don't Panic, But Everything's Wrong." *PC Magazine Online.* 15 December 1996. http://www. zdnet.com.

13. Leyden. "Dawn of a New Renaissance."

14. Vinton Cerf. "Computer Networking: Global Infrastructure for the 21st Century." (database on-line) 1995. available from http://cra.org/research.impact.

15. Bill Gates. *The Road Ahead.* New York: Viking, 1995. 9.

A Guide to News about the Internet, the World Wide Web, and Digital News and Information

Aguilar, Rose. "50 Ways To Go To jail." *CNET.* 14 September 1996. http://www.news.com.

———. "Is the Net Worth It?" *CNET.* 9 September 1996. http://www.news.com.

Aguilar, Rose, and Nick Wingfield. "Users Will Pay to Play." *CNET.* 9 October 1996. http://www.news.com.

"America Online Cuts Staff, Plans a $75 Million Charge." *Wall Street Journal Interactive Edition.* 13 November 1996. http://www.wsj.com.

"America Online Pricing Plan Spurs More Use—and Delays." *Wall Street Journal Interactive Edition.* 12 December 1996. http://www.wsj.com.

"America Online Unveils New, Expanded Advertising Program." *Dow Jones News Service.* 25 June 1996. http://www.wsj.com.

"American Reporter Challenges CDA." *American Reporter.* 8 February 1996. http://www.newshare.com.

"Amer Online Says Role Won't Diminish as Web Use Rises." *Dow Jones News Service.* 19 June 1996. http://www.wsj.com.

Anderson, Scott J. "Confessions of a Multimedia Reporter." 12 January 1997. available from online-news@planetary news.com.

Andrews, Paul. "Sci-Fi Wiz Bruce Sterling Leaps into Future Again." *Seattle Times.* 6 October 1996. sec. C.

Ante, Spencer. "The Blimp That Blazed a Trail Through the Information Skyways." *New York Times on the Web*. 15 November 1996. http://www.nytimes.com.

―――. "With All the Rules Changed, AOL Is a New Ball Game in '97." *New York Times on the Web*. 1 January 1997. http://www.nytimes.com.

Antonucci, Mike. "Age, More Than Income, May Actually Divide the 'Haves' from the 'Have-Nots' in the Digital Age." *San Jose Mercury News Online Edition*. 2 March 1997. http://www.sjmercury.com.

Arnst, Catherine. "Commentary: Power to the States? It Won't Work in Telecom." *Business Week*. 18 December 1995. 85.

Aronson, Karla, George Sylvie, and Russell Todd. "Real-time Journalism." *Newspaper Research Journal*. Summer/Fall 1996. 53–67.

"ATM Description." Ziff-Davis Publishing Company. 9 September 1996. http://www.zdnet.com.

"Attitudes Toward the Media." *Time*-CNN Poll. October 1996. http://www.pathfinder.com.

"AT&T Plans To Shut Down an On-Line Services Group." *Wall Street Journal Interactive Edition*. 23 September 1996. http://www.wsj.com.

Attorney General of the United States v. American Civil Liberties Union et al. no. 96-963. 12 June 1996.

Aubrey, David. "ADSL: Another Pipe Dream." *ZDNet*. May 1996. http://www.zdnet.com.

Auchard, Eric. "IBM Defends Reputation After Olympic Computer Foul-Up." *Reuters*. 27 July 1996.

Auerbach, Jon. "A Primer on the Microsoft Probe." *Boston Globe*. 22 September 1996. http://www.globe.com.

Bank, David. "Instead of Clicking Pages Users View 'Channels' on the Desktop." *Wall Street Journal Interactive Edition*. 13 December 1996. http://www.wsj.com.

Barboza, David. "After the TWA Crash, the Web Proves Its Worth Is Headline Service and Bulletin Board." *New York Times on the Web*. 5 August 1996. http://www.nytimes.com.

Barlow, John Perry, and Bruce Taylor. "To Be or Not To Be (Censored)." *HotWired*. 2 October 1996. http://hotwired.com.

Bartlett, David. "The Soul of a News Machine: Electronic Journalism in the Twenty-First Century." *Federal Communications Law Journal*. 1994. http://www.law.indiana.edu/fclj/fclj.html.

Bass, Bill, and Sara Eichler. "Content Profit Models." *Forrester Research.* 1 May 1996. http://www.forrester.com.

Beatty, Sally Goll. "America Online's Slimmer Focus Targets Tech-Savvy Consumers." *Wall Street Journal Interactive Edition.* 30 September 1996. http://www.wsj.com.

"Berners-Lee Staggered by What People Put Up with on Web." *Technology Review.* July 1996. 32.

Bernstein, Nina. "On Minnesota Prison Computer Files To Make Parents Shiver." *New York Times on the Web.* 18 November 1996. http://www.nytimes.com.

Berst, Jesse. "Five Sure-Fire Internet Fortunes for 1997." *ZDNet AnchorDesk.* 6 January 1997. http://www.zdnet.com.

———. "The Interface That Will Replace Windows." *ZDNet AnchorDesk.* 26 December 1997. http://www.zdnet.com.

Biederman, Christine. "Unsavory Lawsuit Could Test Free Speech in Cyberspace." *New York Times Interactive Edition.* 13 December 1996. http://www.nytimes.com.

———. "When Bomb Blueprints Are Protected Speech." *New York Times on the Web.* 1 August 1996. http://www.nytimes.com.

Biederman, Christine, and Jamie Murphy. "Rebellion Over Who Controls the Net." *New York Times on the Web.* 23 November 1996. http://www.nytimes.com.

Black, Eric. "Q: Are Journalists Liberal? A: Yes." *Minneapolis Star Tribune.* 18 August 1996. sec. A.

BNA Daily Report for Executives. 6 January 1997. sec. A.

Bondi, Richard. "Re: Pictures of murder." 10 October 1996. e-mail to online-news@planetarynews.

Bozdonelos, Nicholas. "Psychology of Computer Use: Prevalence of Computer Anxiety in British Managers and Professionals." *Psychological Reports.* 1996. 995–1002.

Bray, Hiawatha. "Hard-Core Fixes To On-Line Porn." *Boston Globe.* 11 October 1996. http://www.globe.com.

———. "Internet Hackers on the Attack." *Boston Globe.* 20 September 1996. http://www.globe.com.

Brickman, Gary. "New Venture Will Bring Web-Browsing to TV Sets." *Interactive Age.* 11 July 1996. http://www.interactiveage.com.

Brinkley, Joel. "Who Will Build Your Next Television?" *New York Times on the Web.* 28 March 1997. http://www.nytimes.com.

Broder, John, and Laurence Zuckerman. "Computers Remain Unready for the Future." *New York Times Interactive Edition.* 7 April 1997. http://www.nytimes.com.

Brush, Michael. "Wall Street Journal's New Paid Service Tests Web Market." *Money Daily.* 29 April 1996. http://www.pathfinder.com.

Burke, Jonathan. "Internet for the Masses." *Red Herring.* November 1996. http://www.redherring.com.

Bush, Vannevar. "As We May Think." *Atlantic Monthly.* July 1945. http://isg.sfu.ca/~duchier/misc/vbush.

"Cable Modems Sales To Go Up. Up. Up." *USA Today.* 29 May 1996. sec. B.

Calem, Robert. "AOL To Close GNN and Lay Off 300." *New York Times on the Web.* 14 November 1996. http://www.nytimes.com.

———. "Disgruntled MSN Members Launch Site to Air Grievances." *New York Times on the Web.* 23 November 1996. http://www.nytimes.com.

———. "Hackers Vandalize C.I.A.'s Web Page." *New York Times on the Web.* 19 September 1996. http://www.nytimes.com.

———. "Junk E-Mail: Obnoxious and Profitable." *New York Times on the Web.* 20 September 1996. http://www.nytimes.com.

———. "New York's Panix Service Is Crippled by Hacker Attack." *New York Times on the Web.* 14 September 1996. http://www.nytimes.com.

———. "Predicting the Wintel Dynasty's Fall." *New York Times on the Web.* 6 December 1996. http://www.nytimes.com.

———. "TV News: Election Night on the Web." *New York Times on the Web.* 12 November 1996. http://www.nytimes.com.

Camron, Victoria. "Subject: If GM Had Tech Support . . . ." 4 April 1996. e-mail to jhistory@lists.nyu.edu.

"Career Change for Deep Blue." *Information Week.* 27 May 1996. 12.

Caruso, Denise. "Microsoft Morphs into a Media Company." *Wired.* http://www.wired.com.

Cauley, Leslie. "Bell Atlantic Nynex PacTel To Shut Down Tele-TV." *Wall Street Journal Interactive Edition.* 6 December 1996. http://www.wsj.com.

Cerf, Vinton. "Computer Networking: Global Infrastructure for the 21st Century." 1995. http://cra.org/research.impact.

Chesnais, Pascal, Matthew J. Mucklo, and Jonathan A. Sheena. "The Fishwrap Personalized News System." proceedings of the 2nd International Workshop on Community Networking. Princeton, N.J. June 1995.

Clark, Don. "Companies Need Overhauling for the Age of Web Business." *Wall Street Journal Interactive Edition.* 17 June 1996. http://www.wsj.com.

———. "Too Many Web Publishers Vie for Too Few Customers." *Wall Street Journal Interactive Edition.* 14 January 1996. http://www.wsj.com.

———. "Web Ventures Are Shifting Strategies for Local Offerings." *Wall Street Journal Interactive Edition.* 23 September 1996. http://www.wsj.com.

Clark, Tim. "Want To Run a Banner on a Web Page?" *CNET.* 4 October 1996. http://www.news.com.

Clark, Tim, and Jeff Pelline. "E-commerce Fears Persist." *CNET.* 9 October 1996. http://www.news.com.

"Class-Action Suit Filed Against America Online." *Reuters.* 15 January 1997.

Claymon, Deborah. "Not So Fast." *Red Herring.* November 1996. http://www.herring.com.

Clinton, William. "Remarks of the President." 22 February 1993. http://www.whitehouse.gov.

Coates, James. "The Online Grapevine Web Usenet Spawn Flood of Falsehoods." *Chicago Tribune.* 9 November 1996. http://www.chicago.tribune.com.

"CompuServe's Chief Massey Expresses Cautious Optimism." *Wall Street Journal Interactive Edition.* 30 August 1996. http://www.wsj.com.

"Computer Glitch Stalls AT&T's E-Mail Service." *Associated Press.* 8 November 1996.

Conaghan, Jim. "The Conaghan Report: Tracking Audience and Advertising on the Web." Newspaper Association of America. http://www.naa.org.

Consoli, John. "Who's Using the Web? FIND/SVP Survey Results Revealed." *Editor & Publisher Interactive.* 1 August 1997. http://www.medinfo.com.

Corcoran, Elizabeth. "On the Internet, a Worldwide Information Explosion Beyond Words." *Washington Post.* 30 June 1996. sec. A.

Craddock, Ashley. "Texas ISPs Targeted in Secessionist Case." *CNET.* 11 April 1997. http://www.news.com.

"Current Trends." *Wirthlin Report.* August 1996.

"Cyberspace Survey Shows Generation X Getting Politically Active." Tripod. 22 April 1996. http://www.tripod.com.

Davis, Nina J. A. "The Boys in the Bandwidth." *Red Herring.* November 1996. http://www.redherring.com.

deJong, Jennifer. "Are Pioneer Web Advertisers Getting Their Money's Worth?" *Investor's Business Daily.* 15 May 1996. sec. A.

"Diana's Death Interested Everyone." Pew Research Center for the People & the Press. September 1997. http://www.people-press.org.

Dunn, Ashley. "In the Free Web Orchard, Who Will Pay for Fruit?" *New York Times on the Web.* 24 July 1996. http://www.nytimes.com.

"Educator Questions Computers' Educational Value." *USA Today.* 17 July 1997. sec. A.

Eisentadt, Steven. "New Software Blocks Ads on Web." *San Francisco Examiner.* 22 May 1996. sec. B.

"E-mail Goes Bonkers for Epulse." *Sacramento Bee.* 14 June 1996. http://www.nando.net.

Epstein, Edward. "Internet Alters the Art of Campaigning." *San Francisco Chronicle.* 15 October 1996. http://www.sfgate.com.

Evans, David. "1997 May Be Year for Speech Recognition." *Bloomberg Business News.* 30 December 1996. http://www.bloomberg.com.

Evard, Michele. "Children's Interests in News: On-line Opportunities." *IBM Systems Journal* 35 (1996): 412–430.

"Expert Warns of Lax Web Security." *Reuters.* 24 December 1996.

Fabrikant, Geraldine. "Murdoch Bets Heavily on a Global Vision." *New York Times.* 29 July 1996. sec. D.

"FBI Decency Inquiry Criticized in CompuServe Lawsuit." *New York Times.* 11 May 1996. sec. A.

"FCC Unanimously Approves Rules For the Introduction of Digital TV." *Associated Press.* 25 July 1996.

Ferrell, Keith. "Net Apocalypse." *CNET.* http://www.news.com.

Fidler, Roger F. *Mediamorphosis: Understanding New Media.* Thousand Oaks, Calif.: Pine Forge Press, 1997.

"5th WWW User Survey." Georgia Tech University. http://www.survey@cc.gatech.edu.

Fisher, Lawrence. "America Online Crash Unplugs 6 Million Users." *New York Times on the Web.* 8 August 1996. http://www.nytimes.com.

———. "University Internet Proposed." *New York Times on the Web.* 7 October 1996. http://www.nytimes.com.

Fleming, Lee. "Web Broadcasting: An Overview." Gartner Group. http://gartner4.atvantage.com.

Flynn, Laurie. "Lexis-Nexis Flap Prompts Push for Privacy Rights." *New York Times on the Web.* 13 October 1996. http://www.nytimes.com.

"Four Horsemen of the Net Apocalypse." *CNET.* 31 October 1996. http://www.news.com.

Frezza, Bill. "Beware of Geeks Bearing Gifts, Ira Magaziner's Principles." *Communications Week.* 14 July 1997. 51.

Frook, John Evan. "AOL To Launch Promotional Blitz." *Interactive Age.* 17 September 1996. http://www.InteractiveAge.com.

———. "Intel's Net Telephone Strategy." *Interactive Age.* 23 July 1996. http://www.InteractiveAge.com.

———. "New Products Control Bandwidth Usage." *Interactive Age.* 8 October 1996. http://www.InteractiveAge.com.

Frost, Robin. "Web's Heavy U.S. Accent Grates on Overseas Ears." *Wall Street Journal Interactive Edition.* 26 September 1996. http://www.wsj.com.

Gabriel, Trip. "Computers Help Unite Campuses But Also Drive Some Students Apart." *New York Times on the Web.* 11 November 1996. http://www.nytimes.com.

Gaslin, Glenn. "Comdex Redefining the Word 'Nerd.' " *Los Angeles Daily News.* 21 November 1996. http://www.ntysin.com./live/Latest.

Gates, Bill. "Government in the Information Age." *New York Times Special Features.* 18 July 1996. http://www.ntysin.com./live/Latest.

———. "It's Not the Money." *New York Times Special Features.* 22 October 1996. http://www.ntysin.com./live/Latest.

———. "Looking Back at Comdex." *New York Times Special Features.* 3 December 1996. http://www.ntysin.com./live/Latest.

———. "Predictions for 1997." *New York Times Special Features.* 30 December 1996. http://www.ntysin.com./live/Latest

———. "The Online Challenge to Individual Privacy." *New York Times Special Features.* 5 November 1996. http://www.ntysin.com./live/Latest.

———. *The Road Ahead.* New York: Viking, 1995.

———. "TV and PC Will Merge in the Age of the Internet." *New York*

Times Special Features. 11 April 1996. http://www.ntysin.com/live/ Latest.

"Gates Predicts a Wired Africa." Reuters. 6 March 1997.

Gaw, Jonathan. "Internet Snoops." *Minneapolis Star Tribune*. 21 March 1996. sec. A.

"Generation X Examined in Major Study: Media Habits, Beliefs about Morality, Religion, Work, Technology Revealed." American Society of Newspaper Editors. 14 August 1996. http://www.anse.org.

Gentry, Leah. "Buckbobbill: Journalist." Newspaper Association of America. December 1996. http://www.naa.org.

Gilder, George. "Civilization Can't Afford to Forget." *Forbes ASAP*. December 1996. http://www.forbes.com.

———. "Focal Point On Convergence." *Educom Review*. March/April 1995.

———. *Life after Television: The Coming Transformation of Media and American Life*. New York: W. W. Norton, 1995.

Giussani, Bruno. "Mourning Diana: Online Chat Becomes a Book of Condolences." *New York Times on the Web*. 2 September 1997. http://www.nytimes.com.

Glaser, Mark. "E-Zines Find Road to Profits Is Long, Bumpy and Winding." *New York Times on the Web*. 18 October 1996. http://www.nytimes.com.

Glennan, Thomas K., and Arthur Melmed. "Fostering the Use of Educational Technology: Elements of a National Strategy" (database online). 1996. available from http://www.rand.org.

Gomes, Lee. "A Look at Allstate Shows Why Preparing 2000 Is So Tough." *Wall Street Journal Interactive Edition*. 9 December 1996. http://www.wsj.com.

———. "Even New Computer Software May Not Work in Year 2000." *Wall Street Journal Interactive Edition*. 18 September 1996. http://www.wsj.com.

Goodell, Jeff. "The Fevered Rise of American Online." *Rolling Stone*. 3 October 1996.

Green, Heather. "Analyst Lowers Netscape Rating." *Bloomberg Business News*. 18 September 1996. http://www.bloomberg.com.

Greenstein, Jane. "Advertisers Still Trying To Get a Line on Net Users." *Los Angeles Times*. 2 December 1996. http:/www.latimes.com.

Grossman, Lawrence K. "Reflections on Life Along the Electronic Super-highway." *Media Studies Journal* 8, no. 1 (1994): 27–39.

Grumman, Cornelia. "Hate Microsoft? Join the Club." *Chicago Tribune.* 5 June 1996. http://www.chicago.tribune.com.

Gunther, Marc. "The Cable Guys' Big Bet On the Net." *Fortune.* 25 November 1996. http://www.pathfinder.com.

Hafner, Katie, and Matthew Lyon. *When Wizards Stay Up Late: The Origins of the Internet.* New York: Simon & Schuster, 1996.

Harrington, Jeff. "And Now, a Word from Our Sponsor." *Cincinnati Inquirer.* 20 May 1996. sec. A.

Harrington, Mark. Address to Radio and Television News Directors Association. Los Angeles. 10 October 1996.

Harvey, David. "Firms Trace Surfers' Prints as Privacy Debate Heats Up." *Wall Street Journal Interactive Edition.* 2 November 1996. http://www.wsj.com.

———. "On-Line Services Face Threats From Slew of Content Options." *Wall Street Journal Interactive Edition.* 6 July 1996. http://www.wsj.com.

Hatfield, Larry. "Racist Cancelbots Spur Security Fears." *San Francisco Examiner.* 27 September 1996. http://www.sfgate.com.

Heaviside, Sheila, Toija Riggins, and Elizabeth Farris. "Advanced Telecommunications in U.S. Public Elementary and Secondary Schools." National Center for Education Statistics. February 1997.

Hedges, Chris. "Serbian Response to Tyranny: Take the Movement to the Web." *New York Times on the Web.* 8 December 1996. http://www.nytimes.com.

Heilemann, John. "CDA Update." *HotWired.* 20 March 1997. http://www.hotwired.com.

Heskett, Ben. "Gates Preaches PC's Staying Power." *CNET.* 19 November 1996. http://www.news.com.

Heyboer, Kelly. "Computer-Assisted Reporting's 'Dirty Harry.'" *American Journalism Review Online.* June 1996. http://www.newslink.org.

Heyward, Andrew. "Keynote Address." Edward R. Murrow Awards. Radio and Television News Directors Association. Los Angeles. 9 October 1996.

Hilzenrath, David. "Turnaround Task at AOL." *Washington Post.* 31 October 1996. sec. E.

"History of Cyberspace." Cyber History. 28 October 1996. CYHIST@SJUVM.STJOHNS.EDU.

Hoffman, Donna L., William D. Kalsbeek, and Thomas P. Novak. "Internet Use in the United States: 1995 Baseline Estimates and Preliminary Market Segments." University of North Carolina and Vanderbilt University. 12 April 1996.

"HP, Compaq to Invest in Flat Panel Start-Up." *Wall Street Journal Interactive Edition*. 14 May 1996. sec. B.

Hundt, Reed. "A + B = C Access + Bandwidth = Communications Revolution." speech delivered by FCC Chief of Staff Blair Levin. INET Conference. Montreal, Canada. 28 June 1996. http://www.fcc.gov.

———. "Digital TV: We Can Work It Out." speech to the International Radio and Television Society. New York City. 21 November 1995. http://www.fcc.gov.

———. speech to the *Wall Street Journal* Business and Technology Conference. Washington, D.C. 18 September 1996. http://www.fcc.gov.

Huus, Karen. "Indonesia." *MSNBC Online*. http://www.msnbc.com.

"Internet Advertising. Media and Technology Strategies." September 1996. Forrester Research. http://www.forrester.com.

"Internet Market Share Size and Demographics: A Study by Wired." Winston Strategic Information. December 1996. http://www.wired.com.

James, Phil, ed. *Official Netscape Navigator 2.0 Book/Windows Edition*. Research Triangle Park, N.C.: Ventana Communications Group, 1995.

"Japan Sony To Sell Flat-Panel Plasma LCD TV." *Dow Jones News Service*. 30 September 1996. http://www.wsj.com.

Jensen, Elizabeth, and Eben Shapiro. "Murdoch, Turner Trade Jabs. But Can't Afford To Be Enemies." *Wall Street Journal Interactive Edition*. 28 October 1996. http://www.wsj.com.

Johnson, Todd. "Getting a True Picture of What Consumers Are Doing Online." speech to the Advertising Research Foundation Media Research Summit. 24 July 1996.

Jones, Charisse. "Trying To Put the Inner City on the Internet." *New York Times on the Web*. 3 August 1996. http://www.nytimes.com.

"Journalists Are Seen as Arrogant, Aloof." *Milwaukee Journal-Sentinel*. 14 December 1996. http://www.onwisconsin.com.

Kalfus, Marilyn, and Jean Pasco. "Young Adults Are Plenty Optimistic." *Orange County Register*. 25 October 1996. sec. A.

Kane, Margaret. "WebTV Launches New Video Technology." *ZDNet*. 8 January 1997. http://www.zdnet.com.

Katz, Jon. "Bland Ambition." *HotWired*. 3 December 1996. http://www.hotwired.com.

———. "Corporate Suckdogs." *HotWired*. 9 October 1996. http://www.hotwired.com.

———. "Liberally Speaking." *HotWired*. 27 September 1996. http://www.hotwired.com.

———. "No News Is Good News." *HotWired*. 9 October 1996. http://www.hotwired.com.

———. "The Threat From Within." *HotWired*. 7 October 1996. http://www.hotwired.com.

Kelley, Kevin. "Interview with a Luddite." *Wired*. June 1995. http://www.wired.com.

Kirkpatrick, David. "A Look Inside Allen's Think Tank: This Way to the I-Way." *Fortune*. 11 July 1994. http://www.pathfinder.com.

———. "Fast Track at Compaq." *Fortune*. 1 April 1996. http://www.pathfinder.com.

———. "TCI to Announce Joint Venture For Direct-Broadcast Television." *Wall Street Journal Interactive Edition*. 21 October 1996. http://www.wsj.com.

Koprowski, Gene. "InfoCops." *HotWired*. 2 January 1997. http://www.hotwired.com.

Kornblum, Janet. "AOL Plans European Foothold." *CNET*. 4 December 1996. http://www.news.com.

———. "AOL Tightens Grip on Content." *CNET*. 12 December 1996. http://www.news.com.

———. "AOL: Under the Gun Online" *CNET*. 15 January 1996. http://www.news.com.

———. "AOL Users in for Sticker Shock?" *CNET*. 7 November 1996. http://www.news.com.

———. "AOL Warns of Slowdowns." *CNET*. 27 November 27. 1996. http://www.news.com.

———. "Hack Attack Strikes Again" *CNET*. 16 December 1996. http://www.news.com.

———. "Interview with Robert Pittman." *CNET*. 28 April 1997. http://www.news.com.

———. "Is Clinton's Net Access for Real?" *CNET.* 17 October 1996. http://www.news.com.

———. "ISP Battles for Rebels' Rights." *CNET.* 2 May 1997. http://www.news.com.

———. "Online Services Suffer Identity Crisis." *CNET.* 27 December 1996. http://www.news.com.

———. "Private Lives Online." *CNET.* 11 October 1996. http://www.news.com.

———. "To Catch a Hacker." *CNET.* 21 September 1996. http://www.news.com.

Krasner, Jeffrey, and Eric Convey. "AG Probes America Online." *Boston Herald.* 9 July 1996. sec. A.

Krauthammer, Charles. "Downloading the Future." *Washington Post.* 21 June 1996. sec. A.

Krieger, Todd. "Hackers Go on TV to Show Perils in ActiveX." *New York Times on the Web.* 13 February 1997. http://www.nytimes.com.

Krol, Ed. *The Whole Internet: User's Guide and Catalog.* 2nd ed. Sebastopol, Calif.: O'Reilly and Associates, 1994.

Lamott, Anne. "AOL: Agent of Lucifer." *Salon.* 5 August 1996. http://www.salonmagazine.com.

Landler, Mark. "Baby Bells' TV Developers Are on Hold and Frustrated." *New York Times on the Web.* 5 August 1996. http://www.nytimes.com.

Lash, Alex. "Net TVs Not Yet Must-See." *CNET.* 16 December 1996. http://www.news.com.

Lasica, Jay. "Journalism's Challenge in an Interactive Age." *American Journalism Review.* November 1996. http://www.newslink.org.

Lee, Henry K. "Cronkite Pans TV News at Caen Lecture; He Says Internet Presents Society 'Frightful Danger.'" *San Francisco Chronicle.* 13 November 1996. sec. A.

Leibowitz, Wendy. "Lawyers and Technology." *National Law Journal.* 21 October 1996. sec. B.

Lemay, Laura. *Teach Yourself Web Publishing with HTML in a Week.* Indianapolis, Ind.: Sans Publishing, 1995.

Levin, Carol. "Beware the Web Backlash." *PC Magazine Online.* 28 December 1996. http://www.zdnet.com.

Levin, Carol, and Angela Hickman. "Don't Panic, But Everything's

Wrong." *PC Magazine Online.* 15 December 1996. http://www.zdnet.com.

Levins, Hoag. "Newspapers May Lose 14% to Internet." *Editor & Publisher Interactive.* 1 November 1996. http://www.mediainfo.com.

———. "The Online Classified Reports New Cyberspace Advertising Technologies to Impact Newspaper Revenues in 3 Years." *Editor & Publisher Interactive.* 21 November 1996. http://www.mediainfo.com.

———. "Online Gloom in Newspaper Offices." *Editor & Publisher Interactive.* 25 October 1996. http://www.mediainfo.com.

———. "Promise and Threat of WebTV Technology." *Editor & Publisher Interactive.* 8 November 1996. http://www.mediainfo.com.

Lewis, Peter. "Advertising: Technology for the Cybermarketing Age." *New York Times on the Web.* 18 September 1996. http://www.nytimes.com.

———. "An 'All You Can Eat' Price Is Clogging Internet Access." *New York Times on the Web.* 17 December 1996. http://www.nytimes.com.

———. "Free Long Distance Phone Calls!" *New York Times on the Web.* 5 August 1996. http://www.nytimes.com.

———. "I Navigate. You Explore. They Make Money." *New York Times on the Web.* 19 August 1996. http://www.nytimes.com.

———. "Microsoft Plots Ambitious Growth for MSN." *New York Times on the Web.* 11 October 1996. http://www.nytimes.com.

———. "More Users Now Take Direct Route to Internet. Survey Finds." *New York Times on the Web.* 23 September 1996. http://www.nytimes.com.

———. "New Flat Rate Creates Surge in Usage of America Online." *New York Times on the Web.* 3 December 1996. http://www.nytimes.com.

———. "Technology: Talk of Internet's Collapse Greatly Exaggerated." *New York Times on the Web.* 2 September 1996. http://www.nytimes.com.

———. "World Panel Meets to Revise Copyright Laws." *New York Times on the Web.* 2 December 1996. http://www.nytimes.com.

Leyden, Pete. "Dawn of a New Renaissance." *Minneapolis Star Tribune.* 4 June 1995. sec. A.

Little, Darnell. "New Telephony Application May Revolutionize Communications." *Chicago Tribune.* 4 June 1996. http://www.chicago.tribune.com.

"Local Content's Future." Forrester Research. October 1996. http://www.forrester.com.

Lockwood, Lisa. "What Will You Read in 2006?" *WWD.* 24 May 1996. 10.

Lohr, Steve. "The Great Mystery of Internet Profits." *New York Times on the Web.* 17 June 1996. http://www.nytimes.com.

———. "Market Place: America Online. Now on the Big Board. Has Big Plans." *New York Times on the Web.* 17 September 1996. http://www.nytimes.com.

———. "A New Battlefield: Rethinking Warfare in the Computer Age." *New York Times on the Web.* 30 September 1996. http://www.nytimes.com.

———. "Tickling the Ivory and Tweaking the Javascript." *New York Times on the Web.* 9 September 1996. http://www.nytimes.com.

———. "Weighing Costs of Net Access for Every School and Library." *New York Times on the Web.* 21 October 1996. http://www.nytimes.com.

Macavinta, Courtney. "Encryption Policy Challenged." *CNET.* 4 December 1996. http://www.news.com.

———. "Government Service on the Net." *CNET.* 11 February 1997. http://www.news.com.

———. "ISDN: It Still Does Something." *CNET.* 3 December 1996. http://www.news.com.

Machrone, Bill. "Will the Internet Crash?" *PC.* July 1996. http://www.zdnet.com.

Madden, Andrew P. "Coppertunity Knocks." *Red Herring.* November 1996. http://www.redherring.com.

———. "Get Your Kicks on Route 6.1Mbps." *Red Herring.* November 1996. http://www.redherring.com.

Madigan, Charles M., and Bob Secter. "Second Thoughts on Free Speech." *Chicago Tribune.* 4 July 1997. http://www.chicago.tribune.com.

Markoff, John. "Computer Makers to Announce Audio, Video Data Standard." *New York Times on the Web.* 14 October 1996. http://www.nytimes.com.

Markoff, John. "Microsoft Plans Big Rise in Research Spending." *New*

York Times on the Web. 9 December 1996. http://www.nytimes.com.

———. "New Kind of Internet Attack Spreading." *New York Times on the Web.* 19 September 1996. http://www.nytimes.com.

———. "As Technology Spreads Rural Areas Are Not Being Left Out, Study Finds." *New York Times on the Web.* 24 February 1997. http://www.nytimes.com.

McGreal, Rory. "A Snake, Some Oil." *CMC.* 1 September 1995. 7.

McLuhan, Marshall. *Understanding Media.* New York: McGraw-Hill, 1964.

McPherson, Michael. "Geek Humor." 21 May 1996. e-mail to online-news@planetarynews.com.

Meeks, Brock. *MSNBC Online.* 25 April 1997. http://www.msnbc.com.

Memon, Farhan. "The World Wide Wait May Soon Be Over." *Inter@ctive Week.* 7 November 1996. http://www.zdnet.com.

Mendels, Pamela. "Court Says Oklahoma University Can Restrict Internet Access." *New York Times on the Web.* 29 January 1997. http://www.nytimes.com.

———. "Georgia Defends Its Internet Fraud Law." *New York Times on the Web.* 9 November 1996. http://www.nytimes.com.

———. "New Digital Child Porn Law In Budget Bill." *New York Times on the Web.* 3 October 1996. http://www.nytimes.com.

———. "Online Newspaper's Provocation To Test Decency Act." *New York Times on the Web.* 26 April 1996. http://www.nytimes.com.

———. "Study Shows Value of Wired Classroom." *New York Times on the Web.* 26 October 1996. http://www.nytimes.com.

———. " 'Teach-In' Planned for Sunday on New York Online Decency Law." *New York Times on the Web.* 1 November 1996. http://www.nytimes.com.

———. "Youth Group Takes On Site-Filtering Software." *New York Times on the Web.* 28 December 1996. http://www.nytimes.com.

Metcalfe, Robert. "Coming Internet Collapse Spurring Shortsighted Proliferation of Intranets." *InfoWord.* 20 May 1996. http://www.infoworld.com.

———. "Netcom-Cisco Outage Could Foreshadow Much Bigger Collapses Ahead." *InfoWord.* 8 July 1996. http://www.infoworld.com.

———. "With Your Help. I Will Document This Year's Many Internet Collapses." *InfoWord.* 1 April 1996. 48.

239

Meyer, Eric. "All The Newspapers That Fit." *American Journalism Review Online.* 4 June 1996. http://www.newslink.org.

―――. "Online Publishing Continues To Grow Rapidly." *American Journalism Review Online.* April 1997. http://www.newslink.org.

―――. "Predictions for 1997." *American Journalism Review Online.* January 1997. http://www.newslink.org.

―――. "Re: The New Media Reporter." 29 July 1996. online-news@planetarynews.com.

―――. "Stats on Browser Type" 29 August 1996. online-news@planetarynews.com.

―――. "The 10 Myths of Online Publishing." *American Journalism Review Online.* 8 October 1996. http://www.newslink.org.

Miller, Paul. "Zenith Shares Surge as It Wins $1 Billion Digital-TV Contract." *Wall Street Journal Interactive Edition.* 23 August 1996. http://www.wsj.com.

Miller, Thomas. "New Markets for Information." *American Demographics.* April 1995.

Mills, Mike. "Tangle of Computers Adds Up to Simplicity." *Washington Post.* 2 July 1996. sec. A.

"The Promise and Challenge of a New Communications Age." Morino Institute. 15 May 1995. http://www.morino.org.

Morris, Merrill, and Christine Ogan. "The Internet as Mass Medium." *Journal of Communication.* winter 1996.

Mossberg, Walter. "AOL Is Improving Its Service, But Some Problems Remain." *Wall Street Journal Interactive Edition.* 14 November 1996. http://www.wsj.com.

"Move Over CD-ROM." *Popular Science.* July 1996. 25.

Murphy, Jamie, and Charlie Hofacker. "Explosive Growth Clogs the Internet's Backbone." *New York Times on the Web.* 29 June 1996. http://www.nytimes.com.

Negroponte, Nicholas. *Being Digital.* New York: Vintage Books, 1995.

Neuman, W. Russell. *The Future of Mass Audience.* New York: Cambridge University Press. 1995.

"New Twist on Web Advertising." *St. Petersburg Times.* 14 October 1996. sec. A.

"New Web Ad Counting Service In Beta." *Newsbytes.* 13 May 1996. http://www.newsbytes.com.

"Nielsen Internet Demographics Recontact Study." *Media Research Interactive Services*. March/April 1996. http://www.nielsen.com.

Nielsen, Kirk. "New-Old Journalism." *Christian Science Monitor Electronic Edition*. 1 August 1996. http://www.csm.com.

"1996 Voters at a Glance." *Associated Press*. 6 November 1996.

Noble, Christopher. "Salinger Claims 'Proof' on TWA Missile Theory." *Reuters*. 13 March 1997.

Okerson, Ann. "Who Owns Digital Works?" *Scientific American*. November 1996. http://www.sciam.com.

Outing, Steve. "A Contrary View: Infrastructure Will Slow Internet Speed." *Editor & Publisher Interactive*. 11 September 1996. http://www.mediainfo.com.

———. "AOL Browser Trips Up Wall Street Journal Web Users." *Editor & Publisher Interactive*. 4 October 1996. http://www.mediainfo.com.

———. "Case Study: When the Web Is Better at News Than Paper." *Editor & Publisher Interactive*. 6 September 1996. http://www.mediainfo.com.

———. "Newspapers Online: The Latest Statistics." *Editor & Publisher Interactive*. 13 May 1996. http://www.mediainfo.com.

———. "No Clear Profit Strategies for Online Newspapers." *Editor & Publisher Interactive*. 16 December 1996. http://www.mediainfo.com.

———. "Super-fast Cable Modems Sound Great, But." *Editor & Publisher Interactive*. 29 July 1996. http://www.mediainfo.com.

O'Reilly, Tim. "Publishing Models for Internet Commerce." O'Reilly Associates. 19 June 1995.

Paterno, Susan. "Whither Knight-Ridder?" *American Journalism Review*. January–February 1996. 18.

Paul, Lauren Gibbons. "Push Me, Pull You." *PC Week*. 15 January 1997. http://www.zdnet.com.

Paul, Nora. "Content: A Re-Visioning." Speech to Interactive Newspapers '95. 6 February 1995.

Pavlik, John V. *New Media Technology: Cultural and Commercial Perspectives*. New York: Allyn & Bacon, 1996.

"Payments On The Web." Forrester Research. March 1996. http://www.forrester.com.

"PC Homes Up 16% from Last Year." *Wall Street Journal*. 21 May 1996. sec. B.

"PCs Steal Prime Time from TV." Forrester Research. October 1996. http://www.forrester.com.

"Pedophiles Stalk Internet for Victims." *Cable News Network.* 13 September 1996. http://www.pathfinder.com.

Pelline, Jeff. "Say Goodbye to Small ISPs." *CNET.* 26 August 1996. http://www.news.com.

Penenberg, Adam. "Bill Aims at Net Privacy." 16 January 1997. *HotWired.* http://www.hotwired.com.

"People & Technology Strategies." Forrester Research. September 1995. http://www.forrester.com.

Petzinger, Thomas, Jr. "A Morality Tale Emerges From Wild World of Internet." *Wall Street Journal Interactive Edition.* 1 November 1996. http://www.wsj.com.

Pew Research Center for the People and the Press. "One in Ten Voters Online for Campaign." September 1996. http://www.people-press.org.

Powell, Adam Clayton, III. "On-Ramps to the Information Superhighway." *Media Studies Journal* viii (1994): 113–21.

"Publications for Web-Surfers Face Struggle to Stay Afloat." *Chicago Tribune Internet Edition.* 26 May 1996. http://www.chicago.tribune.com.

Purdy, Matthew. "The Eureka Search." *New York Times.* 15 December 1996. sec. A.

Quarterman, John S. "Imminent Death of the Internet?" *Matrix News.* 6 June 1996. http://www.mids.org.

———. "Summary: Third MIDS Internet Demographic Survey." *Matrix News.* March 1996. http://www.mids.org.

Radio and Television News Directors Association (RTNDA). "Profile of the American News Consumer." 1996.

Rafter, Michele. "Clogged Circuits." *Chicago Tribune.* 6 August 1996. http://www.chicago.tribune.com.

———. "Of Bandwidth and Backbone." *Chicago Tribune.* 6 August 1996. http://www.chicago.tribune.com.

———. "Pipeline Problems." *Chicago Tribune* 6 August 1996. http://www.chicago.tribune.com.

Ramirez, Anthony. "No HAL Yet: Artificial Intelligence Visions Underestimated the Mind." *New York Times on the Web.* 13 January 1997. http://www.nytimes.com.

Raysman, Richard, and Peter Brown. "Regulating Internet Advertising." *New York Law Journal*. 14 May 1996. 3.

Reilly, Patrick. "New WebTV Has Sony, Philips Racing to Snatch Holiday Sales." *Wall Street Journal Interactive Edition*. 25 October 1996. http://www.wsj.com.

"Report Opposes Administration's Cryptography Plans." *New York Times*. 31 May 1996. sec. C.

Resnick, Rosland, and Melinda Gipson. "Classifieds in Crisis." *American Journalism Review Interactive Edition*. 23 July 1996. http://www.newslink.org.

"Responses to New Media Producers' Survey." Poynter Institute for Media Studies. March 1996.

"Retail's On-line Advances." Forrester Research. April 1996. http://www.forrester.com.

Rheingold, Howard. *The Virtual Community*. New York: Harper-Perennial Library, 1994.

Ricciuti, Mike. "Hacking Cost Businesses $800 Million." *CNET*. 6 June 1996. http://www.news.com.

Richissin, Todd. "Sharon Lopatka Anonymously Catered to the Sexual Desires of Others over the Internet." *News & Observer*. 3 November 1996. sec. A.

Rickard, Jack. "Microsoft, the Internet, And BillGatus of Borg." *Boardwatch*. May 1996. http://www.boardwatch.com.

Rifkin, Glenn. "3 Young Minicomputer Pioneers Who Are Aging Quite Nicely." *Wall Street Journal Interactive Edition*. 1 July 1996. http://www.wsj.com.

Robichaux, Mark. "Cable-Industry Firms Bet on Internet Profits." *Wall Street Journal on the Web*. 9 September 1996. http://www.wsj.com.

———. "TCI Pulls $125 Million Stake in the Microsoft Network.' *Wall Street Journal Interactive Edition*. 15 November 1996. http://www.wsj.com.

———. "Telecommunications (A Special Report): Cable Connection." *Wall Street Journal Interactive Edition*. 16 September 1996. http://www.wsj.com.

———. "Telecommunications: Companies Gamble on the Internet." *Wall Street Journal Interactive Edition*. 9 September 1996. http://www.wsj.com.

Rodger, Will. "White House Releases Blueprint for Major Net Issues." *Inter@ctive Week Online.* 27 November 1996. http://www.zdnet.com.

Rogers, Everett. *Communication Technology.* New York: Free Press, 1986.

Rozansky, Michael. "Up to Speed." *Philadelphia Online.* 8 August 1996. http://www.phillynews.com.

Russell, Steve, and Joe Shea. *"American Reporter* Challenges CDA." *American Reporter.* 8 February 1996. http://www.newshare.com:9999.

Rutkowski, Anthony-Michael. "Bottom-Up Information Infrastructure and the Internet." keynote address. Founders Day Symposium. University of Pittsburgh. 27 February 1995.

"Sagan Will Step Down as Head of Time's New-Media Division." *Wall Street Journal Interactive Edition.* 25 October 1996. http://www.wsj.com.

Sandberg, Jared. "AOL Is Close to a Deal on Customers' Lawsuit." *Wall Street Journal Interactive Edition.* 8 July 1996. http://www.wsj.com.

———. "At Last, Main Street.com Is Opening for Business." *Wall Street Journal Interactive Edition.* 17 June 1996. http://www.wsj.com.

———. "Microsoft Plans to Spend $400 Million on the Internet." *Wall Street Journal Interactive Edition.* 15 November 1996. http://www.wsj.com.

Savage, Todd. "Print Execs, Citizen Gates Squabble at Confab." *Wired Online.* 30 April 1997. http://www.wired.com.

Schiesel, Seth. "Global Agreement Reached to Widen Copyright Law." *New York Times.* 21 December 1996. sec. A.

Schlacher, Eric, and Colley Godward. "System Operator Liability." *Boardwatch.* April 1997.

———. "How Internet Smut Is Regulated May Depend on Tools To Filter It." *New York Times on the Web.* 24 March 1997. http://www.nytimes.com.

Schlender, Brent. "What Bill Gates Really Wants." *Fortune.* 16 January 1995. http://www.pathfinder.com.

Schwartz, John. "Site-Seers' Guide to Some Way-Out Internet Futures." *Washington Post.* 3 July 1996. sec. A.

Seminerio, Maria. "Is Time Running Out for Commercial Online Services. ISPs?" *PC Week.* 25 October 1966. http://www.zdnet.com.

———. "Survey Finds Users Want Their Internet TV." *PC Week.* 30 October 1966. http://www.zdnet.com.

Shapiro, Eben. "TCI to Trim Work Force, Cut Back on Executive Pay."

Wall Street Journal Interactive Edition. 5 December 1996. http://www.wsj.com.

———. "Time Warner Seeks $300 Million in Additional Cost Reductions." *Wall Street Journal Interactive Edition.* 10 October 1996. http://www.wsj.com.

Shapiro, Eben, and David Kirkpatrick. "TCI Chief Malone Unveils Strategy To Cut Spending." *Wall Street Journal Interactive Edition.* 28 October 1996. http://www.wsj.com.

Shoemaker, Pamela. *Gatekeeping.* Newbury Park, N.J.: Sage Publications, 1991.

"Shielding Your Kids." *Consumer Reports.* May 1997.

Singer, Jane. "Changes and Consistencies: Newspaper Journalists Contemplate an Online Future." paper delivered at the Association for Education in Journalism and Mass Communication. August 1996.

"66.6 Million Households on Net by 2000." *Editor & Publisher Interactive.* 22 November 1996. http://www.mediainfo.com.

"Social Security Administration Shuts Down Web Site." *Reuters.* 9 April 1997.

Sorkin, Andrew. "Ad Revenue on Web Rises in First Six Months of 1997." *New York Times on the Web.* 4 August 1997. http://www.nytimes.com.

"A Special Year-End Issue." @NY. 27 December 1996. http://www.news-ny.com.

Stepp, Carl Sessions. "The New Journalist." *American Journalism Review Online.* July 1996. http://www.newslink.org.

———. "The X Factor." *American Journalism Review Online.* November 1996. http://www.newslink.org.

Stoll, Clifford. *Silicon Snake Oil.* New York: Anchor Books, 1996.

Stuebe, Alison. " 'Internet Alley' Brings Convention to the Web." *New York Times on the Web.* 15 August 1996. http://www.nytimes.com.

"Subscribers Couldn't Get On Amer Online For 45 Minutes." *Dow Jones News Service.* 26 September 1996. http://www.wsj.com.

Sullivan, John. "Student Indicted for Kidnapping Woman He Met Over Internet." *New York Times on the Web.* 20 December 1996. http://www.nytimes.com.

"Survey Shows Generation X Are Politically Active." *SPC Internet News Service.* 23 April 1996. http://satcom.pb.net/spc/intnews.htm.

245

Swisher, Kara. "There's No Place Like a Home Page." *Washington Post.* 1 July 1996. sec. A.

"Talking with George Gilder." *Educom Review.* July–August 1994. "Technology In The American Household." Times-Mirror Center for The People & The Press. November 1995.

"10 Million Young Adults Storm On-Line." Forrester Research. November 1996. http://www.forrester.com.

"Testing the Nation's Cyber-Q." *Newsweek.* 16 February 1995. "Times Mirror Wants 'Dominant Position' on Internet." *SPC Internet News Service.* 9 March 1996. http://satcom.pb.net/spc/intnews.htm.

"Tuning In: Where TV Meets the Net." *@NY.* 1 November 1996. http://www.news-ny.com.

"Turning Content Into Cash." Forrester Research. June 1995. http://www.forrester.com.

"TV News Viewership Declines." Pew Research Center for the People & the Press. 13 May 1996.

University of Washington Libraries. "The Internet: An Overview and Bibliography." Seattle, Wash.: The University, 1994.

"U.S. Online Subscriptions Jump 64% in 1995." *SPC Internet News Service.* 7 March 1996. http://satcom.pb.net/spc/intnews.htm.

"U.S. Government Plans Computer Emergency Response Team." *Chronicle of Higher Education.* 5 July 1996.

"U.S. Toughens Child Pornography Law." *Reuters.* 2 October 1996.

Wallace, David J. "Judge Prevents AOL from Blocking E-Mail." *New York Times on the Web.* 7 September 1996. http://www.nytimes.com.

Walt, Vivienne. "Snooze Control: For Netizens. Elections Weren't Such a Bore." *Wall Street Journal Interactive Edition.* 16 November 1996. http://www.wsj.com.

"Wanted: Ads That Work." *New Media Age.* 14 May 1996. vii.

Watson, Tom. "A City Plan to Wire Schools." *@NY.* 11 July 1997. http://www.news-ny.com.

"The Web in Perspective: A Comprehensive Analysis of Ad Response." I/Pro. 8 October 1996. http://www.ipro.com.

"Web Info Internet Glossary." http://www.info.ink.org.

Weber, Thomas. "Slow Takeoff Suggests WebTV Isn't Ready for Prime Time." *Wall Street Journal Interactive Edition.* 2 January 1997. http://www.wsj.com.

Weber, Thomas, and Jared Sandberg. "America Online President Quits After Only 4 Months at Service." *Wall Street Journal Interactive Edition.* 25 June 1996. http://www.wsj.com.

Weise, Elizabeth. "Software Problem KOs AOL." *Associated Press.* 7 August 1996.

Wells, Rob. "IRS: No Handle on Year 2000 Problem." *Associated Press.* 2 April 1997.

Werbach, Kevin. "Digital Tornado: The Internet and Telecommunications Policy." FCC. 27 March 1997. http://www.fcc.gov.

West, Don. "The Once and Future Cable: Continental Cablevision Chairman Amos Hostetter Interview." *Broadcasting & Cable.* 8 May 1995. 32.

White, Katherine, and Sam Byassee. "Protecting the Franchise: Legal Issues for Electronic Newspapers." paper presented at Connection '96. 14 June 1996.

Williams, Margaret. "New TV Internet System Is Licensed." *Bloomberg Business News.* 10 July 1996. http://www.bloomberg.com.

Wingfield, Nick. "FTC Shuts Down Alleged Pyramid Scheme." *CNET.* 12 November 1996. http://www.news.com.

———. "Giants Step into Streaming." *CNET.* 12 September 1996. http://www.news.com.

———. "Netscape Hears Call of Streaming Audio." *CNET.* 8 November 1996. http://www.news.com.

Woodward, Calvin. "Web Filters Are Kind of Erratic." *Associated Press.* 27 March 1997.

Woody, Todd. "Internet Libel: The Shape of Things To Come." *American Lawyer.* 17 October 1996. 4.

Wresch, William. *Disconnected.* Brunswick, N.J.: Rutgers University Press, 1996.

Young, Peter. "Meet Microsoft's Steve Ballmer, Bill Gates' Alter Ego." *Forbes Online.* 27 January 1997. http://www.forbes.com.

Yovovich, B. G. "Demographics of Web Use." *Editor & Publisher Interactive.* 25 April 1997. http://www.medinfo.com.

Zakaria, Tabassum. "Year 2000 Computer Bug To Cost U.S. Government Billions." *Reuters.* 22 August 1996.

Zimmerman, Phil. "U.S. Senate Testimony on Encryption." 22 July 1996. http://www.thomas.gov.

Zitner, Aaron. "Internet Losses: The Traditional Rules Don't Apply in Running On-line Enterprises." *Boston Globe.* 22 November 1994. sec. A.

Zoglin, Richard. "The News Wars." *Time.* 21 October 1996. 19.

Zuckerman, Laurence. "America Online Moves to Placate Angry Users. *New York Times on the Web.* 17 January 1997. http://www. nytimes.com.

Index

Index

Index

Index

255

About the Author

Christopher Harper worked for more than two decades in the media, including positions with the Associated Press, *Newsweek,* and ABC News.

Harper, the Roy H. Park Distinguished Professor of Communications at Ithaca College, has written extensively about digital media in a variety of publications, including the *American Journalism Review* and *Editor & Publisher Interactive.*

He lives with his wife, Elizabeth, and his daughter, Cecylia, in Ossining, N.Y.